THE PICTORIAL HISTORY OF
COLLEGE FOOTBALL

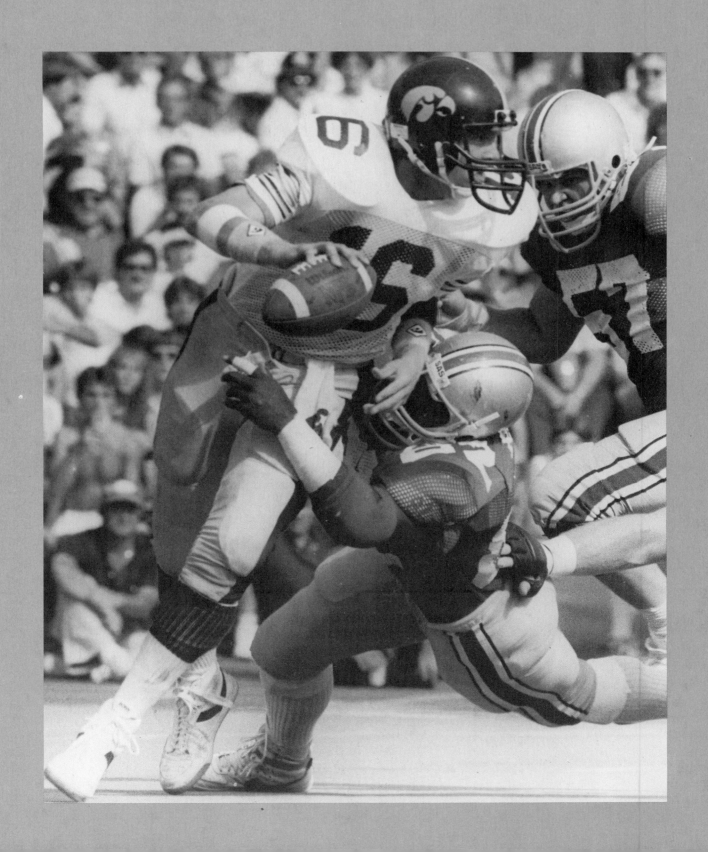

THE PICTORIAL HISTORY OF
COLLEGE FOOTBALL

MELISSA LARSON

GALLERY BOOKS
An imprint of W.H. Smith Publishers Inc.
112 Madison Avenue
New York, New York 10016

Part I
From the Ivy League West: 1869-1910

Part II
There Were Giants In Those Days: 1911-1940

Published by Gallery Books
A Division of W H Smith Publishers Inc.
112 Madison Avenue
New York, New York 10016

Produced by
Brompton Books Corp.
15 Sherwood Place
Greenwich, CT 06830

ISBN 0-8317-6903-3

Printed in Portugal

10 9 8 7 6 5 4 3 2 1

Part III
The Dynasty Years: 1941-1982

Part IV
The Challenge of Modern Times

Introduction

College football belongs to America. Whatever debt we owe to the British for sending over its soccer and rugby forebears, the fact remains that football is uniquely American. Europeans, some of whom would like to believe that everything of value in the US has its roots in the old country, watch professional football games staged in their capital cities, and shake their heads in wonder, so little do they understand how such a game could have evolved.

The imagination to create strategies, new formations, tricky tactics – and the physical talent to make them work – are the fruits of Yankee ingenuity and the strong, quick, aggressive young bodies our country produces in such abundance. But perhaps it is love for a simple game, zest for competition and a yearning for football's particular glories, that gives the game such a hold on our emotions.

The culture that has grown up around college football is also an American product. The color and pageantry provided by cheerleaders, marching bands, mascots, Homecoming floats, tailgate parties, and symbolic trophies lends sophistication and a sense of tradition to the grunts and groans on the gridiron itself. Besides, American spectators don't just want to look on – they want to join in. Thus they wear school colors, sport pins and bumper stickers, sing songs and yell things that would make their parents blush – all in the name of "school spirit."

Today's collegiate game is only one step removed from a professional pursuit. The lure of the pro game and its high salaries, overzealous booster clubs, ambitious coaches and the philosophy of "winning is everything" have obscured some of the high-minded principles of gentlemanly fair play which the Staggs, Heismans and Camps of the game lived by. But we as spectators and fans of the game must help to guard it. As long as there are true fans watching, the game itself must survive.

And as long as there are Homecomings, the alumni will return, lured by their memories. To spend a fall afternoon in a football stadium, watching the Big Game, is to be reminded of our own college days, when we were young and carefree, when there was a bounce in our step and a jingle in our pockets, and when beating the rival school and toasting the inevitable victory was life itself. This book is for you who sat and watched, and jumped to your feet, cheering wildly, and trudged home tired and happy through autumn leaves.

PAGE 1: *Chuck Long of the Iowa Hawkeyes.*

PAGES 2-3: *An autumn day, a packed stadium, and lots of noise and tradition: college football at its best.*

LEFT: *Today's college games pack action and power to spare. Here, the 1987 Gator Bowl match between LSU and South Carolina.*

PART I

From the Ivy League West: 1869-1910

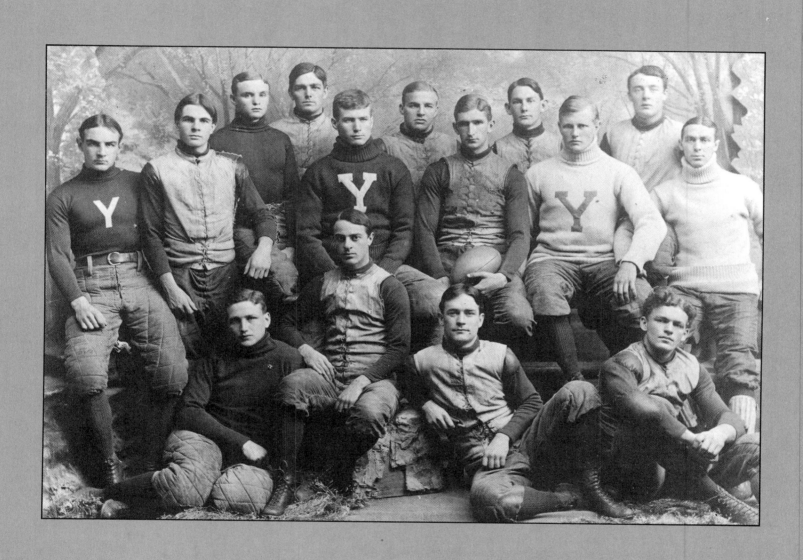

The First Game

Every great invention has an origin. As to the origin of the game of football, however, we are unlikely ever to settle on which ancient culture, society or country is to be credited with "inventing" football. Perhaps it is not even necessary to designate one group for the honor (or blame, as many a football mother would like to). The Greeks may have "gotten the ball rolling" with a game they called harpaston. The Romans also played something like football, complete with an oval-shaped ball (legend has it that they played with a severed human head taken in battle), and the Eskimos, Chinese and Celts are also singled out as having contributed to the grand concept.

The English called their rowdy game a "mellay," the predecessor to the term melee (a near riot), and played the game just as it sounds, as part of their pre-Lenten celebrations. Inflated pig bladders were used as balls at first, before village shoemakers began to fashion more suitable balls from hides.

Actually, it's likely that all of these cultures, and many more besides, played early games involving the moving of a cylindrical object of some sort toward an opponent's goal, with any number of players on either side rolling, hitting, kicking or carrying that object toward the goal. Football, soccer, rugby, basketball, ice hockey, field hockey, lacrosse and many other games derive from that simple, pleasurable concept.

It is battle reduced to a harmless game, in which the winners win

"DRIBBLING" IN ASSOCIATION FOOTBALL.

PREVIOUS PAGE: *Yale team, 1900.*

BELOW: *The game of Rugby, which evolved at the English school of the same name in the 1820s.*

ABOVE: *Association football, a name later abbreviated to soccer, preceded modern football.*

OPPOSITE: *An early ball game.*

only glory, and the losers lose only their pride for a day. Once modern man could concern himself with matters other than feeding, clothing and protecting his tribe and family, he found time to play at battle, and thus perhaps to laugh in the face of his daily struggles for survival.

Of particular note in the early days of the sport was the Oneida Football Club of Boston, established in 1862 and which, according to a stone monument erected in 1925, "played against all comers from 1862-65. The Oneida Goal was never crossed." The monument, on Boston Common opposite the Spruce Street Gate, was unveiled by the seven surviving members of the club. Into the monument is carved what you or I would immediately recognize as a football, complete with stitching. Perhaps by 1925, with football fast becoming a national passion, the seven realized that they had had something to do with making history, and wanted to commemorate it.

By whatever circuitous route, something like football was played between Princeton and Rutgers on 6 November 1869, and is regarded as having been the first intercollegiate football game. The country, torn and bleeding from years of civil war, was ready for diversion, and football games of a sort had been contested from time to time on the secondary school level both in Europe and the US. There were few rules and no organization to the game in America: An inflated balloon-like ball was used and the play probably resembled soccer more than anything else.

The Princeton-Rutgers game grew out of a challenge made by William S Gummere of Princeton, class of 1870, to William Leggett of Rutgers, class of 1872. It was almost inevitable that the two nearby schools would get together for a contest: Each had been playing football for years, and the teams had similar rules.

Legend has it that the two colleges had an annual struggle over an historic cannon that George Washington and Lord Howe had fought over. Princetonians had recently settled the matter forcibly by sinking the cannon into solid concrete on their own campus. So a football match seemed like the next best thing.

Rutgers footballers accepted the challenge of the Princeton men to play three matches, at New Brunswick, Princeton, and New Brunswick, respectively. Since the schools had almost identical rules, the only sticking point was the "free kick." Princeton players were accustomed to having 10 feet, after catching the ball on the fly or first bounce, to attempt a kick at the goal "without hindrance." Rutgers men had no such rule. A compromise was reached whereby the free kick would be allowed at the game played at Princeton, but not at the

ABOVE: *A plaque at Rutgers commemorating the first college football game shows the full name and class year of each participant.*

TOP: *This fine old engraving by Winslow Homer shows a match about to begin "between sophs and freshmen" at Harvard, circa 1857.*

LEFT: *The first intercollegiate football game, Princeton vs. Rutgers, 1869, is depicted in this painting which hangs in the Football Hall of Fame at Rutgers.*

two played at New Brunswick – thus football's first "home-field advantage" was born.

The date of 6 November was set for the first game, and on the appointed morning the Princeton football team of 25 strapping young men, accompanied by "supporters" and other hangers-on, took the train up to New Brunswick. The Rutgers students met them at the station "in a mass, and devoted the day exclusively to their hearty entertainment," according to a later newspaper account.

Old-fashioned hospitality was the rule as the Princeton visitors and their Rutgers hosts strolled around town, played billiards together,

and had lunch – players and fans alike, all in a high state of excitement over the approaching afternoon's activity. Contrast this with the last college football pep rally you witnessed, and you can appreciate the gentlemanly spirit and sense of fair play that characterized these early games.

Meanwhile, team captains Gummere and Leggett, who were to become New Jersey Chief Justice and a distinguished Dutch Reformed clergyman, respectively, carved out the first set of rules for college football. They determined that the field would be 360 feet long and 225 feet wide. Goals were to be 24 feet wide, and marked by simple po‑

Each side would be limited to 25 players. No throwing or running with the ball – a round, inflated rubber thing – or a foul would be called. No tripping or holding of the players was to be allowed. The winner of the first toss would have the choice of position, and the winner of the second would have the first kickoff. Each goal counted one point, and six points were needed to win the game. Lastly, there would be six officials: four judges and two referees.

With the preliminaries taken care of, fans and players headed for the field between upper College Avenue and Sicard Street, where Rutgers Gymnasium is now located. No admission was charged, and both sides performed pre-game college songs, cheers and blood-curdling yells created especially for the event, which left them exhausted but even more excited. Princeton's pre-game yells were supposedly adapted from regimental yells they had heard from soldiers marching through town during the recent Civil War, a sobering forerunner to today's light-hearted, if sometimes profane, college cheers.

Details of the actual game are drawn from an historic account in the new Rutgers student newspaper, the *Targum*. This was the pre-game scene: "Previous to calling the game, the ground presented an animated picture. Grim-looking players were silently stripping, each one surrounded by sympathizing friends, while around each of the captains was a little crowd, intent upon giving advice, and saying as much as possible."

According to accounts, the Rutgers men wore red stocking caps. The combatants took off their hats, coats and vests, the rubber ball was found and play began. Two goaltenders, or "Captains of the Enemy's Goal," were stationed in front of the goal for each team. Their job was to kick the ball toward the opponent's goal if they got their hands on it. Remaining players were organized into squads of "fielders" who patrolled various parts of the field, and "bulldogs" who travelled up and down with the ball. Meanwhile, faithful spectators for each team had seated themselves on the ground out of harm's way.

LEFT: *Princeton's 1873 football team, dressed as proper gentlemen of their era, poses for a formal photo.*

ABOVE: *"A Tackle and Ball Down": football, 1887-style, was a hair-pulling, head-whacking affair.*

Others sat down on the top board of a fence partially surrounding the field.

As play progressed, the rubber ball needed frequent repairs, which stopped play. From accounts in the *Targum*, it appears that each side took turns scoring on their possessions:

To describe the varying fortunes of the match, game by game (play by play), would be a waste of labor, for every game (play) was like the one before. There was the same headlong running, wild shouting, and frantic kicking. In every game (play) the cool goaltenders saved the Rutgers goal half a dozen times; in every game (play) the heavy charger of the Princeton side overthrew everything he came in contact with; and in every action, just when the interest in one of those delightful rushes at the fence was culminating, the persecuted ball would fly for refuge into the next lot, and produce a cessation of hostilities until, after the invariable 'foul', it was put in straight again.

Well, at last we won the match, having won the 1st, 3rd, 5th, 6th, 9th and 10th games; leaving Princeton the 2nd, 4th, 7th and 8th. The seventh game (goal) would probably have been added to our score, but for one of our players who, in his ardor, forgot which way he was kicking, a mistake which he fully atoned for afterward.

What the newspaper account doesn't mention, however, was that the game almost ended prematurely in disaster. Late in the game, as Rutgers was leading 4-2, a kick had sent the ball toward the makeshift fence "bleachers" where the spectators were sitting. Princeton player "Big Mike" Michael and George H Large of Rutgers followed in hot pursuit. Unable to stop themselves, they crashed headlong into the fence and hurled a "seething mass" of spectators to the ground. No one was injured, and the game went on after the two players had regained their breath. With a cheer, and a shout, and a crash, college football was off and running.

Making The Rules

ABOVE: *Harvard's 1875 football team, sporting a team letter. Players were beginning to evolve special ways of dressing, both for protection and to distinguish themselves from the spectators in bowler hats.*

It would be tempting to report that, dating from the first historic game, college football quickly sprang up into the game it is today. In reality, there were still many obstacles to organized football as we know it.

First of all, the game played in 1869 between Princeton and Rutgers resembled soccer much more closely than football, because running with the ball was strictly prohibited. A meeting among representatives from Princeton, Yale, Rutgers, and Columbia on 19 October 1873 at the Fifth Avenue Hotel in New York City made this rule, and a few others, official.

However, another style of college football was also being played in America, at that same time. Harvard, which had been invited to the meeting but failed to attend, was playing what they termed the "Boston Game." Under their rules, which more closely resembled rugby than soccer, the round, rubber ball could be picked up and the carrier could run with it until someone tackled him. Also, Harvard played with only 15 men to a side, not 25. As in many other things, the men of Harvard had their own ideas, felt them to be right, and stuck to them.

Football historians feel that, if Harvard had gone along with its eastern neighbor schools and conformed to the "kick-only" rule, the American game of football would never have been developed, and today male college athletes would be playing soccer.

Unable to agree on rules with any of its American neighbors, the Harvard team looked elsewhere. McGill University of Montreal, Canada had a rugby team which agreed to play a series of games with Harvard. After much diplomacy on both sides, Harvard decided to be gracious hosts and play by the Rugby Union rules. That series paved

OPPOSITE TOP LEFT: *Advertisement for an 1876 contest between Harvard and Yale. One of football's oldest and most famous rivalries was an early favorite with the fans.*

OPPOSITE TOP RIGHT: *This nineteenth-century engraving is entitled "A Long Pass." The forward pass would not be instituted for many more years.*

OPPOSITE BOTTOM: *An 1879 match between Yale and Princeton, drawn by A.B. Frost, shows bowlered officials ready to break up any unnecessary roughness.*

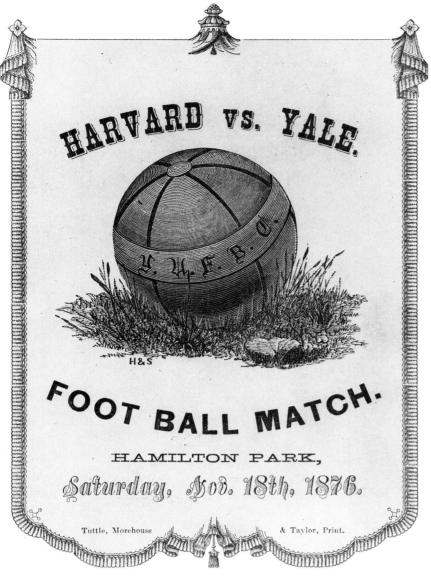

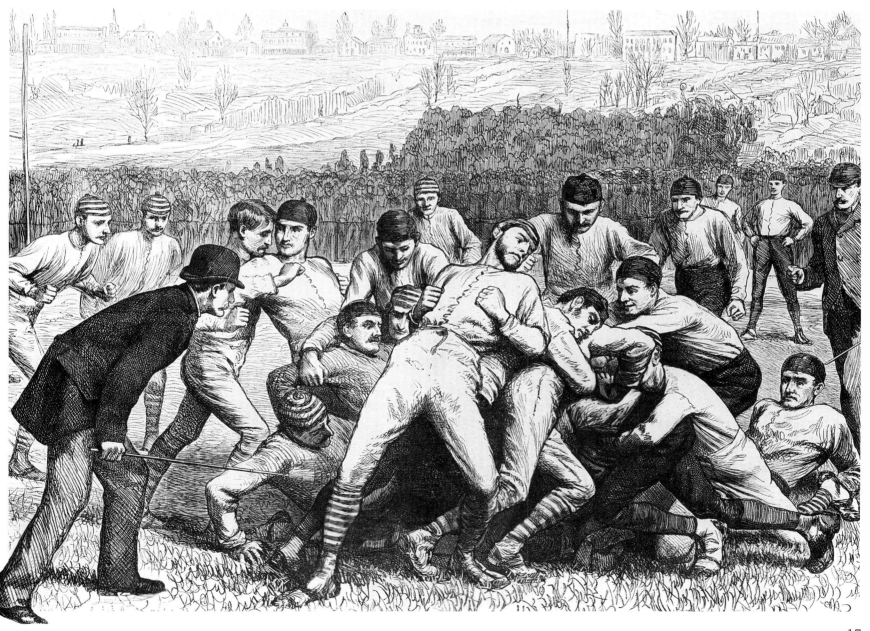

ABOVE: *Harvard football players,*
circa 1875, in a "state of relaxation."   *Note the head handkerchiefs and*
sweaters.

the way for modern American football. Along the way, the two teams began playing with 11 players a side.

A concessionary game followed between Yale and Harvard, at which some of each team's rules were adopted: Thus the first game was played in the classic rivalry of American college football. At that game were two Princeton representatives who liked what they saw so much that they persuaded Princeton to adopt the Rugby Union rules in 1876. At a rules meeting later that year, Yale, Harvard, Columbia and Rutgers agreed to adapt the code of the Rugby Union to their own purposes and to establish what they called the Intercollegiate Football Association.

At that crucial meeting, held at the Massasoit House in Springfield, Massachusetts, it was decided that "a match shall be decided by a majority of touchdowns. A goal shall be equal to four touchdowns, but in the case of a tie, a goal kicked from a touchdown shall take precedence over four touchdowns." The use of an oval ball, rather than a round one, was discussed and adopted. Fifteen players on a side was agreed upon, despite Yale's insistence on eleven. This dispute was one of the reasons that Yale did not actually join the Association until 1879, although it continued to attend meetings and play the member

schools. Yale men continued to lobby for 11-man teams, and won out in 1880.

While the football pioneers of the East were discussing the future, football, in one form or another, was rolling west and south. In 1873, the first intercollegiate game in the South was played between Virginia Military Institute and Washington & Lee. Each squad fielded 50 players. And in 1879, the Midwest ushered in the age of football with a game between the University of Michigan and Racine (Wisconsin) College. Michigan would learn to play the game with some skill in later years.

In those years, the first signs of uniforms were also showing up here and there. Harvard players wore sweaters and tied handkerchiefs around their heads in their games with McGill. McGill footballers wore white trousers, striped jerseys and "turbans." What those must have looked like has been lost in the mists of time.

That was the game of American college football by 1880. Then, along came a man named Walter Camp.

Walter Camp: Father of Football

The true founder of American football was Walter Chauncey Camp, who grew up in Yale University's hometown of New Haven, Connecticut. He first entered Yale at the age of 17 in 1876, intending to finish undergraduate work, enter Yale's law school and become a doctor. Fortunately for the game, football got in the way of that ambition.

It is Walter Camp who weaned American football away from its rugby origins and made it a unique sport. He created the line of scrimmage, the official 11-man team, the practice of calling signals, and the position of quarterback. In addition, he lobbied for tackling below the waist, and originated the rule requiring that a team surrender the ball unless it had advanced at least five yards (now 10) by the fourth down. He also designed a scoring system that eventually evolved into today's point values for touchdowns, extra points, field goals and safeties.

It is difficult to overemphasize Walter Camp's contribution to football. From his undergraduate days as a halfback at Yale, beginning in 1876 until his sudden death – at a rules committee meeting – in 1925, he was the ultimate football authority. Along with his friend Caspar Whitney, he began choosing football's All-America team in 1889, and although other individuals and committees eventually published their own All-America team lists, Camp's was considered the standard.

After leaving Yale in 1884 and spending a few years with the New Haven Clock Company, during which time he continued as an active member of the Intercollegiate Football Association Rules Committee, Walter Camp returned to Yale as its first head football coach. Until that time, Yale football teams, and all others that we know of, were coached after a fashion by the captain of that team.

Camp's position was unpaid, but while he was Yale's coach, he continued to create and establish football and coaching practices which would influence the game. Among them was the practice of using still photographs to study the individual play of his athletes, and eventually of the competition as well.

Another measure of Camp's influence was the number of Yale players who went on to establish brilliant football coaching careers of their own. Among them were Amos Alonzo Stagg, the University of Chicago's famous coach; Minnesota's Henry Williams; and Howard Jones, the stunningly successful football mentor at both the University of Iowa and the University of Southern California.

In 1880 Camp was instrumental in replacing rugby's "scrummage," where the ball was tossed in between two packs of rushers, with the

BELOW: *Walter Camp (center, with ball), as he appeared on Yale's 1879 team. He was the true founder of college football.*

LEFT: *Penn vs. Princeton, 1892. Princeton footballers were known as "Tigers" from the early days when they began sporting striped orange and black sweaters. That may have been the first team nickname.*

OPPOSITE: *Walter Chauncey Camp, football's first great innovator, decked out full length in the uniform of an 1870s Yale football player. He was both coach and captain in 1879.*

RIGHT: *This rare early photo of an 1893 Dartmouth College game shows the chalk lines marked every five yards on the field. Camp instituted the "gridiron" effect so that forward progress could be measured more easily.*

"scrimmage" as a means of putting the ball in play. The scrimmage rule read as follows:

A scrimmage takes place when the holder of the ball puts it on the ground before him and puts it in play while on side, either by kicking the ball or by snapping it back with the foot. The man who first received the ball from the snapback shall be called the quarterback and shall not rush forward with the ball under penalty of foul.

This relatively simple but far-reaching change established football as a game of possession and made it different from rugby, where a team could advance 10 or 20 yards before putting the ball up for grabs again. If a team could possess the ball, it could devise strategies and tactics for advancing the ball - and that was the thing Camp liked best about football. In a time of war, he might have made a brilliant general, but since the nation was at peace, he created a game instead.

In a later interview with famous sportswriter Grantland Rice, Camp described what he called Yale's "Camp System":

At the end of a season I'd call a meeting at which we'd determine who was graduating and who wasn't. Then we'd screen the returnees. Were they fast? Did they pack power? The type of material we would

have pretty much determined our mode of offense. We moved the ball with more authority because, as a team, we worked much harder on signals than our adversaries. As far as I know we also had the distinction of being the first team to develop the cutback – where a back starts at one point in the rival line and hits at another. This got us many, many yards. Remember, however, that everything and anything we tried in those days was new.

Camp wrote three books on the game he loved: *Football: How to Coach a Team* (1886); *American Football* (1891); and *Walter Camp's Book of College Sports* (1893). They were considered gospel in their time.

Camp did not always have his way immediately with the Rules Committee. It took several years for him to prevail at establishing the 11-man-team rule, and his proposal to establish the five-yards-in-three-downs rule in 1882 was questioned as impractical. How, they asked him, would anyone know when five yards had been made?

"We shall have to rule off the field," Camp replied, "with horizontal chalked lines every five yards."

"Gracious!" Princeton representative Ned Peace reportedly said. "The field will look like a gridiron!"

"Precisely," said Camp.

Real Iron Men

LEFT: *Notre Dame's 1896 team, ready for action.*

BOTTOM: *This woodcut shows fashionably-dressed spectators enjoying the 1881 Yale-Princeton game at the New York Polo Grounds.*

OPPOSITE TOP: *As this woodcut by Frederic Remington depicts, football was a brutal game at the turn of the century. Serious injuries were common.*

OPPOSITE BOTTOM: *Yale's flying wedge developed as a weapon against Princeton. Tackles and guards surrounded the ball carrier after the ball was snapped, and dealt swift punishment to the opposition.*

The men who played college football in its early days were big, strong and tough by the standards of their day. Six-footers were the rule, and near the turn of the century a man six feet tall was considered large. Early football players were also wiry and athletic. Most early players were either three- or four-sport athletes in college, like Walter Camp (who played baseball, swam, played tennis, hurdled and rowed crew for Yale) or they were sons of farmers or tradesmen and were accustomed to hard work.

College football in its early days was hard work. The length of the field had been established at 110 yards, which favored long running plays, and all team members played both offense and defense. There were 45 minutes to a half instead of 30. Two games were usually played each week – Wednesdays and Saturdays. Once the game started, a player could not leave unless he was hurt – although inventing injuries was a frequently-used tactic when a captain wanted to bring in a fresh player.

There were no helmets or pads in those days. Teams wore jerseys or shorts, with snug-fitting canvas jackets over them, thus earning the nickname "canvasbacks." Today's players, some of whom shave their heads on the first day of training camp, will be amused by the fact that old-time players grew their hair long to protect their heads – and sometimes grew beards as well.

John W Heisman, after whom the Heisman Trophy is named and who played five years of football at Brown and Pennsylvania, said:

Hair was the only head protection we knew, and in preparation for football we would let it grow from the first of June. Many college men of that day, especially divinity and medical students, permitted their beards to grow. Often they were referred to as 'Gorillas'. . . .

We didn't have many sweaters in those days, but we all wore snug-fitting canvas jackets over our jerseys. You see, the tackling in that day wasn't clean-cut and around the legs as it is today. All too often it was wild, haphazard clutching with the hands, and when runners wore loose garments, they were often stopped by a defensive player grabbing a handful of loose clothing. Some players wore pants, or jackets, of black horsehair. When you made a fumble grab, you lost your fingernails.

In the old days, players of one side were permitted to grab hold of their runners anywhere they could and push, pull or yank them along in any direction that would make the ball advance. Sometimes two enemy tacklers would be clinging to the runner's legs, and trying to hold him back, while several teammates of the runner had hold of his arms, head, hair, or wherever they could attach themselves, and were pulling him in the other direction. I still wonder how some of the ball carriers escaped dismemberment.

Practices could also be brutal. Tackling dummies were unheard of. Yale's team, which set the standard in the early years, prohibited dummies, contending that tackling flesh-and-blood players in practice was the only way to learn how to do it in a real game. Practice scrimmages were hair-pulling, shin-cracking affairs where players vied for the attention of coaches and captains, and often injuries were inflicted on the home team before the opponents even got a chance.

Yale's chief opponent every year was Princeton, with its newly-developed V-wedge or "V-trick." The ball-carrier formed the apex and put the ball in play to a runner, who was screened by the wedge players. Broken teeth, broken bones and bleeding head wounds were inflicted on many of Princeton's foes who tried to stop the V-wedge. Soon Harvard had instituted what it called the "flying wedge," and the principle of mass momentum had spread throughout the game. Legend persists that college players were killed in such games – some say as many as 25 men by the turn of the century. Soon the wedge would be outlawed, but in the late 1880s, football was still a raw and untamed wilderness.

Into this brutal world of college football stepped Yale's great Pudge Heffelfinger in 1888.

Yale and Heffelfinger

LEFT: *Yale's greatest team, the mighty 1888 Elis. Pudge Heffelfinger is in the back row in the middle. With the ball and the handlebar moustache is Captain William "Pa" Corbin. Also on the team, and destined for football immortality: Amos Alonzo Stagg (farthest left).*

OPPOSITE: *William Walter "Pudge" Heffelfinger, the Minnesotan who became college football's first star player. He actively played football until the age of 65.*

By the 1880s football as a spectator sport had become socially acceptable. As rough and brutal as the game was at that time, ladies could attend and root their chosen team on to victory – providing they hid their eyes and threatened to faint if the play got too violent. Crowds of up to 40,000 people had attended games between Princeton and Yale in New York City, and college football had spread throughout the country.

The eastern schools were the dominant teams in football. Princeton, Yale, Harvard, Pennsylvania and other, smaller schools in the East introduced the new plays, fielded the top teams, and received virtually all of what press coverage there was at the time.

In 1888, a freshman named William Walter Heffelfinger from Minnesota reported for football practice at old Yale field. The game was not new to the raw-looking young man, since he had organized a team at his high school, and starred as a back, after reading about the exploits of Yale, Harvard and Princeton in *Spaulding's Guide*. He had also played some exhibition games for the University of Minnesota, long before there were rules prohibiting students his age from playing college ball. At 6ft 3in and 188 pounds, he was ready for Eli football – or so he thought.

Yale also knew a little something about "Pudge" Heffelfinger, as he was called. At one of his first freshman practices, the lanky youth returned a punt and ran through the opposition, impressing Pa Corbin, the varsity captain. Corbin, whose word was law and whose handlebar moustache and advanced age (he was 24) commanded respect, decreed that Pudge would be allowed to try out for Yale's varsity football team.

Corbin directed him to try his talents as a guard on the line. "We need linemen more than backs," he explained. "Have you any nickname?"

"No," replied Heffelfinger, remembering that his father disliked his nickname of "Pudge."

"Fine," said Corbin. "We'll call you 'Heff'. Your real name is too long." They also called him Pudge, not only at Yale but for the rest of his life.

Heffelfinger was to find out what many a young man has discovered

before and since – that freshmen get a rough initiation in football. Early on, the older Yale players were intent on combining the young giants' natural athletic skills with the mental temperament for the kind of football they played.

"You're too good-natured, Heff," counselled one of his Yale linemates. "You've got to be mean to play on this team, and you must bang 'em down hard." In later years, Pudge remembered reminding himself, "You've got to play football for all there is in it, or somebody who hits harder will send you off on a stretcher."

So Pudge Heffelfinger, one of college football's first star players, took his place on the Yale varsity team of 1888, which was regarded as one of the best Yale ever produced. Besides captain Pa Corbin and Heffelfinger, the team boasted two other talented players who would have a considerable influence on the game: Amos Alonzo Stagg, future coach of the University of Chicago, and George Woodruff, who would later coach Pennsylvania to fame.

As for Heffelfinger, he played for Yale from 1888 to 1891, making Camp's All-America list the last three of those years. He then played football for another 45 years, remaining as tough as iron at a top weight of 245, from his senior playing weight of 201. A gifted storyteller, he reminisced in later life:

Some of my sportswriting friends have been kind enough to call me the greatest football player of all time. Naturally, I like to read that sort of thing. But deep in my heart I know it isn't true. I can honestly claim that I stuck with the game longer than anyone else did. On and off, I was an active football player for 50 years.

I started as a fifteen-year-old schoolboy in my home town of Minneapolis, when rugby had just been modified to suit our Yankee yen for knocking people down. I ended as a tired old man of sixty-five in a charity game at Minneapolis against kids old enough to be my grandsons.

But he never lost his zest for football, for as he told sportswriter Joe Williams, "Joe, a game that can keep you so young and vibrant and all steamed up is a precious thing."

The First All-Americans

OPPOSITE: *Walter Camp, who along with his friend Caspar Whitney chose the first All-America team in 1889. His annual choices for All-America honors were considered official until his death in 1925.*

RIGHT: *Yale's football team produced three 1889 All-America players: Pudge Heffelfinger at guard (back row, third from right), tackle Charles Gill (second from right), and end Amos Alonzo Stagg (not pictured here).*

BOTTOM: *Rugged but smiling Hector Cowan of Princeton was another member of that first All-America team, at tackle.*

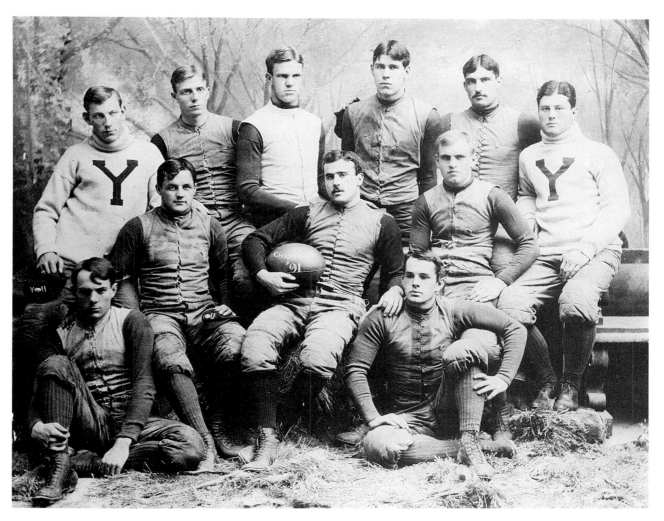

Toward the end of the century, football was well on its way to being the "king of college sports." By 1895 the Western Intercollegiate League, the forerunner of the Big Ten, was born. In the Southwest, a special brand of football, emphasizing the flashy aerial game, was being played at such schools as Texas Christian University. At Wisconsin, kicker Pat O'Dea was thrilling Badger crowds. And Yale alumnus Amos Alonzo Stagg had begun his coaching reign at the University of Chicago.

Beginning in 1889, Walter Camp and close friend Caspar Whitney, who wrote at the time for a New York periodical called *The Week's Sports*, began choosing a team of "All-Americans." These were the best college football players in the nation at each position.

Many credit Camp with conceiving of and starting the All-America team, but sports historians are now convinced that Whitney first had the idea, and picked the first team, with Camp's help. It was published in *The Week's Sports* in 1889, and here were the picks:

Position	Player	School
E	Amos Alonzo Stagg	Yale
E	Arthur Cumnock	Harvard
T	Hector Cowan	Princeton
T	Charles Gill	Yale
G	Pudge Heffelfinger	Yale
G	Jesse Riggs	Princeton*
C	William George	Princeton
B	Edgar Allan Poe	Princeton
B	Roscoe Channing	Princeton
B	Knowlton Ames	Princeton
B	James Lee	Harvard

In later listings of All-America teams under Walter Camp's name, John Cranston of Harvard appears at guard. The following year he made the team unanimously at center. Evidently there was a disagreement between Camp and Whitney over this pick.

Let's take a look at those first All-Americans. Amos Alonzo Stagg was, of course, a standout end on the crushing Yale team, and later went on to influence college football profoundly as Chicago's coach, mentor and guiding spirit for decades. Arthur Cumnock, one of the best ever to wear Harvard's crimson, was the other end chosen. As

Harvard's captain, he would later institute some innovations in preparing his team for the Yale game: a spring practice, and the use of tackling dummies.

Princeton's tackle Hector Cowan was a key player in the Tigers' newly-developed V-wedge. He was a raw-boned farm boy with a battle-axe jaw and enormous arm strength. At the other tackle position the choice was Charles Gill of Yale, a hard-boiled fighter with steely eyes. Yale guard Pudge Heffelfinger was a living legend who went on to play football until he was in his sixties. At the other guard position was perhaps the only man Heffelfinger ever faced who was just as tough – Jesse Riggs of Princeton. The damage these two did to each other during Princeton-Yale games made spectators wince. Princeton's mustachioed William George took honors at center.

Backs on that first All-America team were Edgar Allan Poe, Roscoe Channing, Knowlton Ames, and James Lee. Poe was one of Prince-

ton's six famous Poe brothers, all of whom lettered on Princeton football teams from 1884 to 1900, and three of whom were first-rate players. Edgar was one. He was also the grandnephew and namesake of the famous poet. His teammates Bob Channing and Knowlton "Snake" Ames were also on the team. Channing excelled on runs from the dreaded V-formation, and Ames was, as his nickname implies, a sinuous dodger with a zigzag running style that kept opponents in fits.

The 1890 All-America team was also published in *The Week's Sports*. The following year, Whitney's 1891 picks appeared in *Harper's Weekly*. By 1897, after Whitney had gone abroad, Walter Camp began making the picks under his own name for *Harper's*, also adding second and third teams. Two years later, Whitney returned to *Harper's* and Camp began making picks for *Collier's* magazine.

Camp's choices, published by *Collier's*, were considered official until his death in 1925, when the great sportswriter Grantland Rice

took over the choice of the teams for *Collier's* until 1947. The All-America Board of Coaches, meanwhile, had been making All-America picks from 1924 to 1955. Associated Press and United Press International had also gotten into the act. The Football Writers Association picked an All-America team beginning in 1944. Today, a player voted as a "consensus" All-American means that he has appeared on every recognized All-America team listing at his position – a great honor.

Camp's early selections were overwhelmingly from eastern schools, and the very best players from western, southern and mid-western schools cracked the All-America teams only very slowly over time. But remember that nationwide sports press was unheard of in the early days, and no one could attend two games at once to scout players. Today, televised games and the influential football writers in each geographical region help determine an individual player's selection – based far less on one or two men's personal opinions and biases.

ABOVE: *Princeton's Knowlton "Snake" Ames, a standout back on Camp's first list.*

LEFT: *Harvard's 1890 team picture shows Captain Arthur Cumnock holding the ball and, farthest left in the back row, back James Lee. Both were 1889 All-Americans.*

Heisman, Warner, and Stagg: Inventing Strategy

ABOVE: *Amos Alonzo Stagg, coach and inspiration to scores of U. of Chicago football players.*

OPPOSITE: *Stagg was an outspoken critic of any improper influence on amateur athletics.*

Three coaches of this era, with very different styles and personalities, were to influence the way the game was played for all time. They were Amos Alonzo Stagg, Glenn S "Pop" Warner, and John William Heisman.

Knute Rockne once said, "All modern football stems from Stagg," and few would disagree with him. At the University of Chicago, where he coached for 41 years, Stagg instituted things we now take for granted in football: the diagrammed playbook, the huddle, backfield shifts, men in motion, onside kicks, fake kicks and reverses, just to name a few.

Stagg was a fierce competitor and had the benefit of playing against other outstanding coaches and teams, such as Fielding Yost's Michigan teams, and Bob Zuppke, Red Grange's coach, at nearby University of Illinois. But he also cared deeply for his players as people, and was an outspoken critic of gambling on college games, crooked coaches and managers, and most of all, professional football – which he believed would ruin the sport through corruption of college players.

He believed in clean living – never drinking, smoking or swearing. He had rejected a promising career in baseball after graduation from Yale because he didn't agree with the sale of alcohol at the games. "The whole tone of the game was smelly," he asserted.

Stagg never swore at his players, even when sorely grieved. If a player made a bad mistake, the coach might call him a "jackass" or even a "double jackass" – the worst censure Stagg could bestow. Honor and sportsmanship were more important to him than winning, and he tried his best to communicate that to his players.

His stunning success as a coach is borne out in these statistics: he was the winningest coach in college football history, with 314 victories, until Bear Bryant and Eddie Robinson came along generations later.

Stagg was awarded Coach of the Year honors in 1943, at the age of 81, at the College of the Pacific in Stockton, California, where he had gone when forced to retire from the University of Chicago at age 70. On the occasion of his widely-celebrated 100th birthday in 1962 he said, "I would like to be remembered as an honest man."

Glenn Scobey Warner was known to the football world as "Pop." Next to Stagg, he was the winningest coach ever, until Bear Bryant. In coaching tenures at Georgia, Cornell, Carlisle, Pittsburgh, Stanford and Temple, his record was 313 victories, 106 losses and 32 ties. Pop Warner was never strongly associated with one team, as are most other famous coaches, but he was supremely successful nonetheless.

He was also an innovator. Pop Warner introduced the single wing and double wing formations, in the early years of the forward pass. He also created the spiral punt, rolling body blocks, the use of numbers on players' jerseys, and blocking dummies. But perhaps his greatest claim to fame was that he coached 47 consensus All-Americans, one of whom is recognized as one of football's greatest athletes – Ernie Nevers of Stanford. Another may have been the greatest football player of all time – Jim Thorpe.

Like Stagg, Pop preached good sportsmanship. "You cannot play two kinds of football at once, dirty and good," he said. He also placed a high value on effort. Once asked to compare Nevers to Thorpe, Warner gave the overall edge to Nevers, saying that Thorpe had not always given his best effort. "I'll take the all-outer over the in-and-outer every time," he said. What coach would disagree?

Warner's Pitt teams went undefeated for four straight seasons from 1915 to 1918, and by the early 1920s his fame had spread to the West Coast, where Stanford officials became interested in him. It was there, where he coached from 1925 to 1932, that Warner had some of his greatest players, and where he became involved in the rivalry which haunted him – with the University of Southern California under Coach Howard Jones.

Warner's Stanford team won the first two games in the series and tied the third, but USC took the next five contests. It was his inability to beat Southern Cal which caused Warner to resign from Stanford at the end of the 1932 season. He moved on to Temple, a decision he later characterized as a mistake, and indeed his teams never achieved stardom there. Left behind at Stanford was Coach Tiny Thornhill who, along with his players, became known in football lore as the "Vow Boys," having pledged never to be defeated by USC.

Warner coached until 1938, when he was 67 years old, and is regarded as one of the most influential coaches in the history of college

football. So great was his instructional leadership that today many youth football leagues are called "Pop Warner Leagues" in his honor.

If you can imagine a stern, bespectacled clergyman or college professor with a deep, austere voice, you can imagine John William Heisman. Heisman was actually a short and rather stumpy man, but perhaps no other coach of his day could so mesmerize new recruits or throw the fear of God into them.

Born in the same year as the game he loved, 1869, Heisman first played high school football at 17 against the wishes of his father, who considered the game "bestial." For the next 50 years, Heisman lived football, playing for three years at Brown and then, in 1892, giving up the study of law and beginning his coaching career at Oberlin College. Like Warner, Heisman was a traveller, coaching at eight schools before he retired.

The hidden ball trick, double lateral passes, and the division of the game into quarters were all advocated by Heisman. In addition, he campaigned tirelessly for the legalization of the forward pass, which finally was instituted in 1906.

After coaching at Oberlin and a one-year stint at Akron, Heisman

OPPOSITE LEFT: *Glenn Scobey "Pop" Warner was a great football innovator and preached good sportsmanship above all.*

OPPOSITE RIGHT: *John William Heisman, after whom the Heisman Trophy is named, is best known as Georgia Tech's coach, although he also coached at Oberlin, Akron, Auburn, Clemson, Penn, Washington and Jefferson, and Rice during his long career. He favored long practices and no hot-water baths.*

LEFT: *Pop Warner with Stanford's All-American Ernie Nevers, whom he considered his best player ever.*

BELOW: *Heisman (right) with assistant coach F. Harold Gaston.*

moved on to Auburn for five years, then to Clemson for four seasons, then on to Georgia Tech, where he ruled football for the next 16 years. Heisman was a stern taskmaster and brooked no opposition from his players. He favored long practices and strict training rules. These included a prohibition against hot-water baths and soap during the week (he considered them "debilitating"). Players were also subject to long team lectures, which often included quotes from Shakespeare, delivered in his booming stage voice.

He also invented the "Heisman shift" while at Georgia Tech. This involved the entire team except the center dropping behind the line of scrimmage. The four backs formed a letter "T" at right angles to the rush line. It was one of the most influential early shifts in college football, and quite effective.

Heisman moved on again in 1920, this time to Pennsylvania for three seasons. Washington & Jefferson lured him away in 1923, and he moved to Rice the following year, where he remained until 1927, when he retired at the age of 60.

Heisman's all-time record is an impressive one: 185 victories, 70 defeats and 17 ties. Also, by the time he retired from football he had twice been elected president of the American Football Coaches Association, and was one of the founders of the New York Touchdown Club.

When he died in 1936, the Downtown Athletic Club of New York named its annual award for player excellence, begun the year before, for him – and the Heisman Trophy it's been ever since.

Perhaps those who remember Heisman at his fire-and-brimstone best were his first-year recruits. Heisman traditionally began the season of coaching (and lectures) with this little bit of motivational magic. Holding up the football, he would ask rhetorically, "What is it?"

"A prolate spheroid, an elongated sphere," he would answer himself in his melodramatic tones. "One in which the outer leathern casing is drawn up tightly over a somewhat smaller rubber tubing."

Then, as a hush fell over the group of energetic young players, he would fix them with his most severe ministerial glare and slowly intone, "Better to have died as a small boy than ever to fumble this football."

Football Is Saved

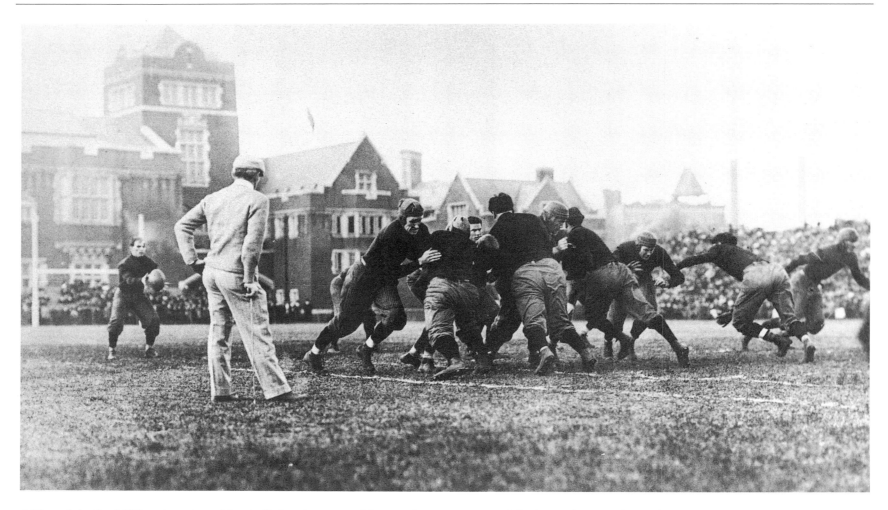

Although in the 1890s adoration of football, its players and its coaches was already springing up in nearly every part of the nation, in reality organized college football was on the brink of doom.

According to no less a football historian than Amos Alonzo Stagg himself, by 1893 nearly every college football team was using some form of the flying wedge, or mass momentum plays. By the end of that season, injuries and general roughness had wreaked such havoc that the Army-Navy game was called off for 1894, the Intercollegiate Football Association was breaking up (only Yale and Princeton now remained in it), and the game itself was falling into disfavor with its fans.

At the end of the 1893 season, a hastily-called meeting among Harvard, Yale, Princeton and Pennsylvania outlawed flying wedge plays

TOP: *Penn-Lafayette game, 1909.*

LEFT: *"Out of the Game, 1891": Drawing depicts grievous injuries which were common in the 1890s. Most historians agree that as many as two dozen players may have died in those days in college football games.*

and reduced the length of the game from 90 to 70 minutes. Yet the group did not outlaw all "mass" plays as such – and by the start of the 1894 season coaches had come up with new formations called "guards back" or "tackles back," which employed heavy guards smashing through the opposing line in tandem. Penn teams, coached by George Woodruff, employed it with stunning success – in fact it might be said that the mass formation put Penn football on the map.

But bitter feelings persisted between teams whose players were being seriously injured – and even killed – in these games. In 1894, the "Big Four" football colleges met again, and split over the issue of mass formations. Princeton and Yale voted to outlaw all mass plays, while Harvard and Penn voted to retain them. Unable to resolve the split, the four schools produced two independent sets of rules.

Meanwhile, in the Midwest, the forerunner of the Big Ten Conference was being formed by its first seven members: Michigan, Wisconsin, Minnesota, Illinois, Chicago, Northwestern, and Purdue. One of the first issues discussed among the members of the new alliance was mass formations.

For the next 11 years, until 1905, each season saw new formations built to smash through opposing lines without compromising the letter of the law, under whatever set of rules was governing that particular game. Each coach devised his own "shift," and it was usually named for him or for the school.

Thus, the Minnesota shift, devised by Dr Harry Williams at Minnesota, the Heisman shift, and others. Each new season brought its rules conferences, during which this or that new rule would be agreed upon in an attempt to stem the violence – and incidentally introduce other innovations. Three-year playing limitations, abolition of the training table, touchdowns counting for five points, and outlawing of coaching by substitutes, all came about during the 1890s.

Yet the mass plays continued. Why? Because football games had already become symbolic tests of bravery – even more so because college players, still without any head protection, were literally risking their lives for their teams. And some of them were indeed killed, or crippled. Stagg later wrote, "The *Chicago Tribune's* compilation for the 1905 season showed 18 dead and 159 more or less serious injuries." Many schools were suspending football altogether: Columbia, Northwestern, and Stanford among them.

In 1905, the public furor had reached the point where President Theodore Roosevelt, himself an avid sportsman, summoned representatives of Yale, Harvard and Princeton to the White House and laid down the law. Football must clean up its act. "Brutality and foul play should receive the same summary punishment given to a man who cheats at cards," the President reportedly said.

Chancellor Henry M McCracken of New York University, who was

also appalled by the violence, convened a conference of college representatives to decide whether football should be reformed or abolished altogether. At the first meeting, on 9 December 1905, 13 eastern schools participated. The second meeting, on 28 December, drew 62 schools, and a Football Rules Committee of seven members was appointed.

They organized themselves as an educational body calling itself the Intercollegiate Athletic Association of the United States, "to assist in the formation of sound requirements for intercollegiate athletics, particularly football." In 1910 it changed its name to the National Collegiate Athletic Association. Merging with the older American Football Rules Committee, headed by Walter Camp, the group adopted programs that opened up the play and reduced the hazards. They had faced the challenge, and saved the game.

TOP: *President Theodore Roosevelt, himself an avid sportsman, deplored football's violence and called for reform.*

LEFT: *This fanciful cartoon appeared in* Harper's Weekly *of 6 November 1889. Entitled "Foot-ball of the Future," it depicts players doing battle in medieval armor.*

Yost's Point-A-Minute Michigan

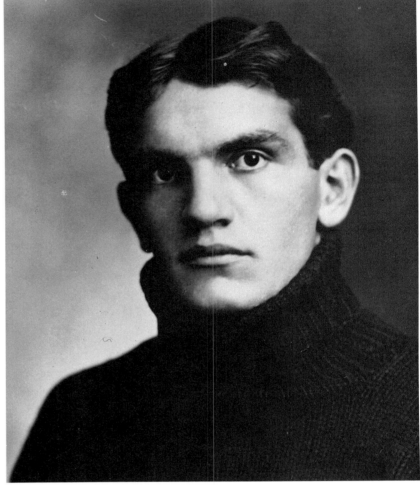

LEFT: *Fielding Yost, coach of the "Point-a-Minute" Michigan Wolverines.*

ABOVE: *Adolph "Germany" Schultz, 1907 All-America center at Michigan.*

OPPOSITE TOP: *The 1901 Wolverines scored 550 points that season, or roughly "a point a minute."*

OPPOSITE BOTTOM: *Willie Heston, star back of Yost's 1901 Wolverines.*

With the new century came new faces, new coaches and teams. An early football dynasty was forged at the University of Michigan under the legendary Fielding Yost, beginning in 1901.

Today's Michigan fans are accustomed to manhandling the Big Ten. They seem to see it as their divine right. But they have relatively short memories. Many who claim to be true Wolverine fanatics remember no further back than Tom Harmon. But before Bo Schembechler, Tom Harmon and Forrest Evashevski – even before Fritz Crisler and Bennie Oosterbaan – there was "Hurry Up" Yost.

Fielding Harris Yost, born in West Virginia in 1871, came to coach at Michigan after successful one-year stints at Stanford, Ohio Wesleyan, Nebraska and Kansas. Yost earned the nickname "Hurry Up" for his emphasis on team speed. He was known to admonish his players constantly to move faster. "Ya think we got all day? You look like a spectator out there! Hurry up! Let's go! Hurry up!"

From the day Yost arrived at the Ann Arbor campus, bringing three of his top players from California, he emphasized speed over brute strength. This was a new concept for the Big Ten, and indeed for college football as a whole.

Willie Heston was one of the players Yost brought along to bring his particular brand of football to Michigan. Heston, who is ranked among

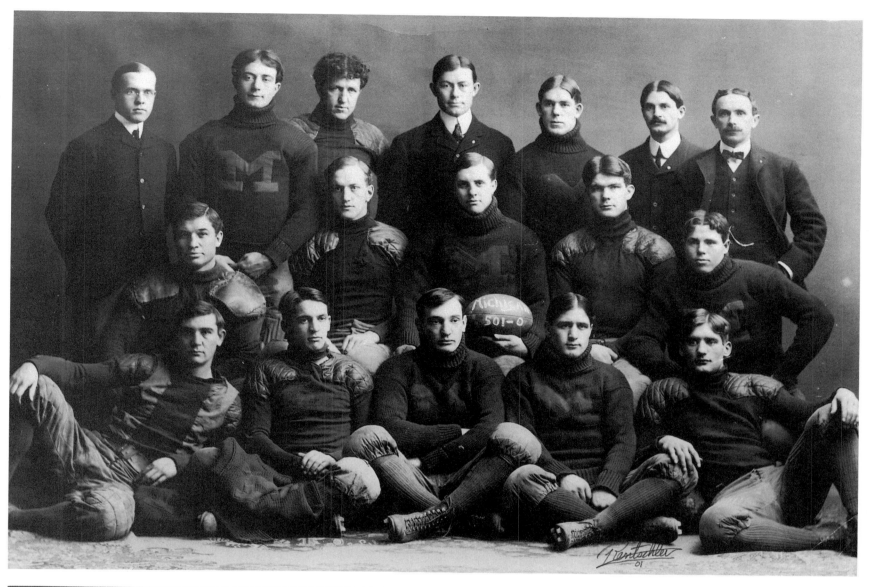

the greatest backs of all time, later had this to say about Yost's effect on the game:

He brought to Michigan an entirely new brand of football, not known to the Big Ten or to the Middle West. Particularly, that was true of his offense. Speed and more speed was continually emphasized. (Quarterback) Boss Weeks was instructed to call his signal for the next play while the team was getting up from the last play.

The linemen would jump into their respective positions, the quarterback would start giving another signal, but the first number was the starting signal. The center would instantly snap the ball, the line would charge, and the play was off. This system would usually catch the opposing team flat-footed.

Yost's 1901 Wolverines, with star back Heston, became known as "Point-A-Minute" Michigan. They racked up scores against opponents that are almost incomprehensible to today's fan – 107 points over Iowa, 86 over Ohio State, 128 points over Buffalo. The Point-A-Minute machine achieved 8000 yards in offense that year for 550 points – one for virtually every minute of play – and finished a perfect 11-victory season by beating Stanford 49-0 on New Year's Day, 1902. It was intended to be the finale to the Festival of Roses in Pasadena, California – the first Rose Bowl game.

Heston was a two-time All-America during his years as a Wolverine, and still makes most football historians' all-time best teams. Thickset yet incredibly speedy, Willie was spoken of almost reverentially by sportswriters. Grantland Rice called him "as hard a man to stop as football has ever known."

Incidentally, because of the truly appalling score achieved against beloved Stanford by Michigan (which graciously allowed the game to end at that score with eight minutes left to play), the Pasedena festival officials called off the "Rose Bowl," as they had named it, for the next 16 years – preferring events such as chariot racing as the capper to the festivities.

Although the Wolverines racked up a total of 55 consecutive vic-

ABOVE: *Fielding H. "Hurry Up" Yost, circa 1927, poses with the spoils of war: a new Packard given to him by grateful alumni, and Michigan's new football stadium. He coached until 1926, then became athletic director.*

OPPOSITE: *A rare photo of Yost, circa 1925, in headgear next to captain and quarterback Benny Friedman. Yost picked the 1925 team as his best ever.*

kind of thing that convinces boosters of other schools that life is not, strictly speaking, fair.

As for Yost, he was remembered with great fondness by players and fans alike: For his West Virginia accent, which he never lost, for his habit of lecturing players (even when he met them by chance on campus) about the right way to play their position, and by his truly rousing pre-game peptalks, which from all accounts rank among the best ever. Willie Heston recalled:

He would tell his boys that the entire Michigan alumni, in fact the whole football world, were awaiting the final result of the game. . . . As the squad was leaving the dressing room to take the field, he would say, "Who are they to beat a Michigan team? They're only human." By this time every player was in a state of mind to seek raw meat.

tories over the next five years, it is the 1901 team which is usually mentioned as perhaps the greatest Michigan team ever. But other tremendous athletes, such as top center Adolph "Germany" Schultz and Tug Wilson, played for Yost in those years.

Yost himself, who was to coach at Michigan until 1926, surprised writers later in his career by picking the 1925 team as his personal "best ever." The 1925 Wolverines boasted end Bennie Oosterbaan and quarterback Benny Friedman, the famous "Benny to Bennie" aerial duo.

Gentle arguments about which team is the greatest of all time are the fans' privilege at such football juggernauts as Michigan. It's the

Yet Yost, a tireless after-dinner speaker, frequently spoke of the importance of the "four-sided man," as he called it. Brains, heart, courage and character, he would say, made up the best athletes – and the most useful citizens. For Hurry-Up Yost, football was a game, a religion, and a way to mold young men.

The First Homecoming

It's difficult to think of a time before there was Homecoming – that traditional stampede back to youth enjoyed every year by alumni – but it wasn't until 1910 that the first Homecoming took place. Credit for the idea goes to two seniors at the University of Illinois.

Elmer Ekblaw and C F Williams were nearing graduation and sentimentally wondering if they would ever return to Champaign. They hit upon the idea of designating one fall weekend – built around an Illini football game, of course – during which alumni would be invited back to renew acquaintances and cheer on the old Orange and Blue. It seemed like such a good idea that they gathered the backing of Illinois' honorary societies and fraternities, and approached the school authorities.

Permission was given to try a "Homecoming" weekend the following fall. Publicity for the event must have been energetic indeed, for on 15 October 1910, almost 5000 Illinois graduates gratefully returned to campus to cheer on the Illini as they beat the University of Chicago Maroons 3-0. Other activities planned that weekend for the entertainment of the returning supporters included a hobo parade and a stunt show.

ABOVE: *Pennsylvania's Truxton Hare, four-time All-American at guard (1897-1900), and forerunner of all great Penn football players.*

OPPOSITE TOP: *A rare photo of the 15 October 1910 game between Illinois and Chicago: the first Homecoming game.*

RIGHT: *Frank Hinkey, Yale's "living flame" and four-time All-American at end.*

OPPOSITE BOTTOM: *A dropkick wins it for Illinois. Almost 500 alumni watched the game.*

As Illinois fans and other football lovers looked back that autumn of 1910, they must have marvelled at the changes that had taken place since 1869. A game had been borrowed and re-invented, so to speak, with rules continuously evolving and the level of play improving by leaps and bounds. As players and coaches experimented with the young game, new strategies and tactics were constantly emerging.

Fans must have thought that there couldn't be any wiser coaches, any more powerful teams, any more exciting players than the ones they knew. They had seen, or read about, such players as Pennsylvania's lineman Truxton Hare, who could drag five tacklers several yards, but whose popularity as a gentleman equalled his talents on the gridiron.

They had heard the legend of Yale's "living flame," four-time All-America end Frank Hinkey, about whom it was said that he had the greatest fighting spirit of any football player to step onto the field. And as recently as 1908 they had thrilled to the exploits of Harvard's great tackle, Hamilton Fish, who anchored the 1908 Crimson line, which many called the best ever.

But fans would find that the best was yet to come. The game had become established, and the stage was set for the wonders of some of its greatest names. Jim Thorpe, Red Grange, Knute Rockne, The Four Horsemen of Notre Dame, Amos Alonzo Stagg, Bronko Nagurski and Tom Harmon are a few of the legendary players and coaches who would leave their marks on the game in the following decades.

LEFT: *Notre Dame's first Homecoming, against Purdue. Football was poised for its greatest years.*

ABOVE: *Australian-born Pat O'Dea, Wisconsin's sensational turn-of-the-century kicker.*

43

PART II

There Were Giants In Those Days: 1911-1940

The Immortal Jim Thorpe

He was born James Francis Thorpe in 1888, near Prague, Oklahoma, of Native American descent. He ended his days having set the football world on its ear, in both the college and professional ranks. Add his incredible feats in the 1912 Olympic Games and his professional baseball career, and it's no wonder that many sports historians still rank Thorpe as the best all-round athlete of all time.

Thorpe's college football feats seem even more unbelievable because he accomplished them at a little place with about 250 students called Carlisle Indian School in Cumberland County, Pennsylvania. Along with Carlisle's legendary coach Pop Warner, Jim Thorpe put the tiny institution on the map and struck a blow for athletic respect for Native Americans as Carlisle teams took on, and defeated, some of the great eastern universities which had dominated college football.

Warner ranked his Carlisle teams of 1907, 1911 and 1912 as the best. Not coincidentally, Jim Thorpe appeared on all three teams, although he only subbed on the 1907 Indians. Even as a substitute, however, he caught Warner's eye:

Thorpe started his football career during the fall of 1907 when he went in as a substitute. He showed considerable ability on his first try. In the following year he was a regular and began to attract attention as a ballcarrier and kicker. At that time he weighed around 178 and was an exceptionally well-built athlete. He had speed as well as strength. He knew how to use his strength and speed as well as any football player or track athlete I have ever known. He was a great competitive athlete and always did much better in actual competition than in practice.

In the spring of 1908 Thorpe made the track team, his specialty being jumping and hurdling. He continued to improve each year and was a great track star when he finished his five-year term in the spring of 1909.

As the term of his enrollment was concluded, Thorpe returned to his home in Oklahoma. We heard no more of Thorpe until the fall of 1911 when the Olympic Games were being discussed. I thought if he would return to school he would stand a very good chance of making the American Olympic team and wrote him to that effect.

He took my advice and, returning to Carlisle, played great football during that 1911 season. The Carlisle team of that year was one of the best which the school ever turned out, defeating both Harvard and Pennsylvania and losing only one game.

Thorpe kicked four field goals against Harvard that year – from the 22-, 15-, 34- and 48-yard lines. He also scored a touchdown as Carlisle handed Harvard a stunning defeat, 18-15. The Carlisle Indian players had to be versatile, and, as Warner recalled, "As for kickers, every man knew what to do with his toe." However, Thorpe, at 6ft and 190 pounds, was far more than just a versatile player. Not only could he do everything on the football field, but it also seemed he did it better than anyone else.

The 1912 season was to be an even bigger one for Thorpe and the Indians. John Heisman later wrote in *Collier's*, "At Carlisle in 1912 that Indian scored 25 touchdowns and 198 points. No player has equalled that. Jim had everything. He was a star punter, a star drop kicker, a star passer. At blocking and end running certainly we've not produced his master."

Perhaps it was the Army game of 1912 that engraved the image of Jim Thorpe into the nation's football consciousness. Army had a stingy defense, but fans had heard something of the Indians and Thorpe, and neither team was heavily favored. Army held its own in the first half with a touchdown by Cadet halfback Leland Hobbs (incidentally, another Army halfback who was playing that day was Cadet Dwight D Eisenhower).

In the second half, however, Jim Thorpe dominated. The *New York Times* reported next day:

Standing out resplendent in a galaxy of Indian stars was Jim Thorpe, recently crowned the athletic marvel of the age [at the Olympics in Stockholm, Sweden]. The big Indian captain added more lustre to his already brilliant record, and at times the game itself was almost forgotten while the spectators gazed on Thorpe, the individual, to wonder at his prowess. . . . He simply ran wild while the Cadets tried in vain to stop his progress. It was like trying to clutch a shadow.

Thorpe went through the Army line as if it were an open door. His defensive play was on a par with his attack. . . . Thorpe tore off runs of 10 yards or more so often that they became common. . . . In the third period he made a run which . . . will go down as one of the greatest ever seen on the Plains. . . . [Catching a punt on Army's 45-yard line] Thorpe, zigzagging first to one side and then to the other, wormed his way through the entire Army team.

PAGE 45: *In the huddle: Fordham's 1933 team.*

OPPOSITE: *James Francis Thorpe, reckoned by many to be one of the greatest athletes of all time. He is pictured here in the football uniform of the Carlisle Indian School in 1909.*

ABOVE: *Thorpe as he appeared in the line with professional football's New York Giants, 1925.*

LEFT: *Among the most versatile players of all time, Thorpe was a sensational punter and kicker.*

Unfortunately, the score was called back for a Carlisle penalty. Yet the final score was Carlisle 27, Army 6. Not since 1900 against Harvard had a team scored as many points against Army. Losing coach Ernest Graves said that he had just witnessed the finest offensive attack of his career.

The 1912 season was Thorpe's last at Carlisle. He had made Walter Camp's All-America teams in both 1911 and 1912 at halfback, and had just finished winning gold medals in both the pentathlon and decathlon. All the world was singing his praises. Yet misfortune was just around the corner for the Sac and Fox Indian.

Charges of professionalism – specifically a summer playing baseball with the Rocky Mount Club in the Eastern Carolina League in 1909, for an "insignificant" amount of money – were proven and the United States Olympic Committee apologized to the world and sent back Thorpe's medals and trophies, worth almost $50,000. His Olympic records were erased.

Fifteen years playing professional football, and seven years in the major leagues playing baseball for John McGraw's New York Giants (mostly on the bench) added to his legend, but the humiliation of having his Olympic medals stripped always rankled with the proud Indian.

Recently, however, Thorpe's descendants were awarded honorary Olympic medals in his name by the United States Olympic Committee, in recognition of his achievements and also, perhaps, in atonement for an injustice, since today's athletes are allowed to compete as amateurs in Olympic games even if they are professional in another sport.

Grantland Rice wrote in 1936, "All the wild laurels you can gather for the pick of the past in football belong to Jim Thorpe. The answer to this is simple – Thorpe could do more things well, even up to the point of brilliance, than any other player in the game."

The Forward Pass Takes Off

While the nation had been cheering Jim Thorpe, other schools and teams were winning glory and advancing football as a modern sport. Strong teams in 1911 included Pennsylvania, Minnesota (conference champs under Dr Harry Williams), Chicago, Wisconsin, Vanderbilt, Georgia, Texas, Notre Dame, Army and Dartmouth.

In 1912, Princeton and Yale fielded good teams, along with Georgetown, Texas Christian, and Swarthmore. Undefeated Wisconsin won the Big Ten that year, and Notre Dame was also undefeated. This Notre Dame team was the same one which would achieve fame the following year in the game against Army – the game which, say the historians, ushered in the forward pass.

Starting in 1912, the game had taken on a fundamental similarity to modern football. The touchdown had been given the value of six points, and the length of the field had been reduced to 100 yards, with 10-yard end zones behind each goal line. Perhaps most important, teams were now allowed four downs instead of three to gain the 10 yards needed for a first down. Structurally, then, the molding of the modern game had essentially been completed.

But most football scholars still look back at the 1913 Notre Dame-Army game as the event which unleashed the pass, although it had been used, in one form or another and with varying degrees of success, for at least seven years.

Notre Dame teams had played football in relative obscurity until this time – as hard as that may be to comprehend. Not until quarterback Gus Dorais began throwing the football to end and captain Knute Rockne, and little Notre Dame crushed mighty Army, did the football world know where South Bend, Indiana was – and what the forward pass could do. Incidentally, that 1 November 1913 game also kicked off one of football's great rivalries.

Harry Cross described the legendary game this way in the *New York Times*:

The Notre Dame eleven swept the Army off its feet on the Plains this afternoon and buried the soldiers under a 35-to-13 score. The Westerners flashed the most sensational football that had been seen in the East this year, baffling the Cadets with a style of open play and a perfectly developed forward pass, which carried the victors down the field 30 yards at a clip. . . .

The yellow leather egg was in the air half the time, with the Notre Dame team spread out in all directions over the field waiting for it. The Army players were hopelessly confused and chagrined before Notre Dame's great playing, and their style of old-fashioned, close, line-smashing play was no match for the spectacular and highly-perfected attack of the Indiana collegians.

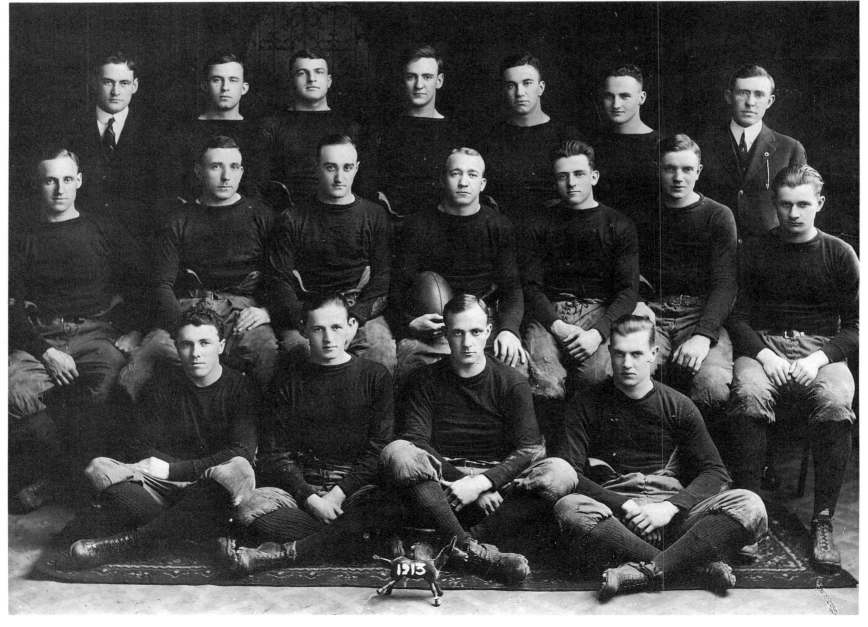

OPPOSITE: *Notre Dame's 1913 team photo shows a young, determined Knute Rockne holding the ball (center).*

TOP: *Fritz Pollard of Brown University (back row, right) was the first black to make Camp's All-America list (1916).*

ABOVE: *The Notre Dame team, led by Knute Rockne, trots out onto the field for the 1913 opening game against Ohio Northern.*

Not long before his death, Knute Rockne, who would become Notre Dame's beloved coach and achieve lasting fame, reminisced in the *New York World* in 1931 about what it had taken to win the game in 1913:

We took it (the pass) up the instant we saw it. Dorais . . . and I spent a whole summer vacation at Cedar Point on Lake Erie. We worked our way as restaurant checkers and what not, but played on the beach with a football, practicing forward passing . . . .

The Notre Dame-Army game also seemed to spark a new era for coaches. It was as if the possibilities of the forward pass loosened a torrent of new strategic ideas in such innovators as Bob Zuppke at Illinois, Amos Alonzo Stagg at Chicago, Mike Donahue at Auburn, and others.

Another trend had started as well, and Harry Cross may have sensed it when he referred to the Fighting Irish as "the Westerners." Football had energized every corner of the Midwest, which had strong, big-boned young men in abundance. And it had talented coaches, many of them former eastern players with a hunger to spread the football word. While the eastern establishment went on about the business of running the government and anticipating a world war, the game of football became an all-consuming passion in the Midwest.

TOP: *Army's 1913 players: Notre Dame's rival in the famous game which ushered in the forward pass.*

LEFT: *Knute Rockne, captain of the Fighting Irish, before the 1913 Army game.*

OPPOSITE: *Crowds thronged outside this shop to hear a radio broadcast of the Notre Dame-Army game.*

ABOVE: *Rockne's quarterback in that famous game, Gus Dorais. The two Notre Dame players made the forward pass a reality.*

New Conferences

The decade 1910-20 also saw the official organization and development of regional football conferences across the country. In 1914 came the founding of the Southwest Conference, with eight charter members: Arkansas, Baylor, Oklahoma, Oklahoma A & M (now Oklahoma State), Rice, Southwestern, Texas, and Texas A & M. In late 1915 the Pacific Coast Conference, which would become the PAC-10, was formed, with charter members California, Oregon, Oregon State, and Washington.

These newcomers joined the eastern schools (who would not offi-cially be known as the Ivy League until 1954), the Big Ten, and the Southern Intercollegiate Athletic Association (SIAA, the forerunner of both the Atlantic Coast Conference and the Southeastern Conference). The SIAA had been founded in 1894 with charter members Alabama, Auburn, Georgia, Georgia Tech, Sewanee and Vanderbilt. Also organized was the Missouri Valley Intercollegiate Athletic Association, which had begun in 1907 and by 1908 boasted Iowa, Kansas, Missouri, Nebraska, Washington University, Drake and Ames College (later Iowa State).

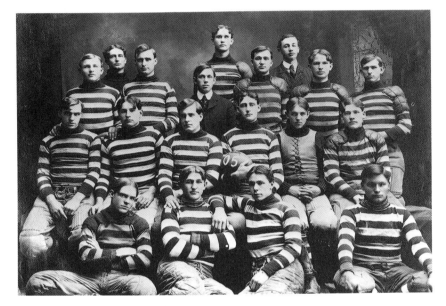

OPPOSITE TOP LEFT: *Oklahoma's 1905 football team: College football had spread to the heartland.*

OPPOSITE TOP RIGHT: *Princeton's 1922 Tigers: the "Team of Destiny."*

OPPOSITE BOTTOM: *Yale University cheerleaders, circa 1925.*

ABOVE: *USC and Cal were already duelling over supremacy on the West Coast. Here, Gus Shaver's (USC) punt is blocked in a 1931 contest.*

RIGHT: *Charley Trippi, Georgia's great back, steaming 65 yards for a touchdown in a game against Georgia Tech, 1946. The SIAA was the forerunner of both the Atlantic Coast Conference and the Southeastern Conference.*

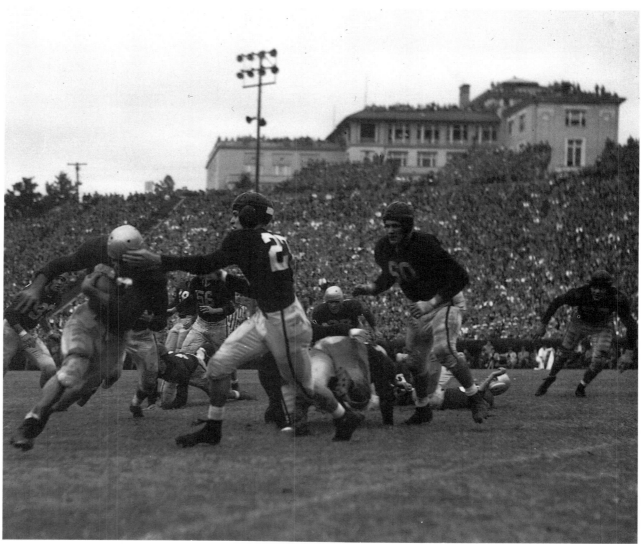

RIGHT: *The start of an end run during a Columbia-NYU game in the 1930s. Local rivalries were a hit with the fans from the beginning, and would become a practical necessity during World War II when unnecessary travel was restricted.*

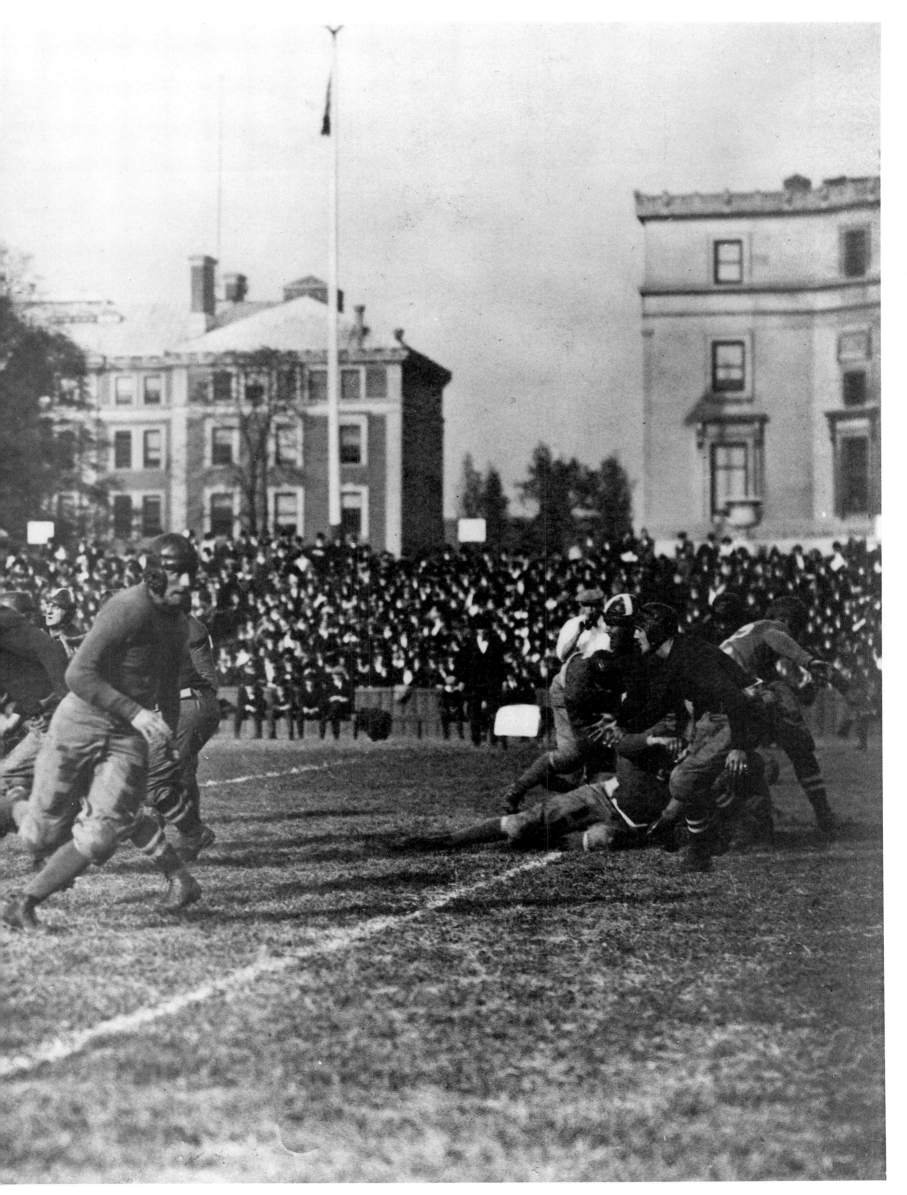

RIGHT: *This early Rose Bowl contest (1917) pitted the University of Oregon against mighty Penn, with Oregon an upset winner, 14-0. Penn is in striped jerseys, Oregon in the plain.*

BOTTOM LEFT: *A poster advertising the game between Brown and Washington State in Pasadena on New Year's Day, 1916. The Rose Bowl has been an institution ever since.*

BOTTOM RIGHT: *Texas A & M football became well-known around 1917 under coach Dana X. (Xenophon) Bible.*

OPPOSITE BOTTOM: *"Gloomy Gil" Dobie's coaching record at Washington between 1908 and 1916 was 58-0, yet he was so universally disliked that even Huskie fans regularly pelted him with fruit.*

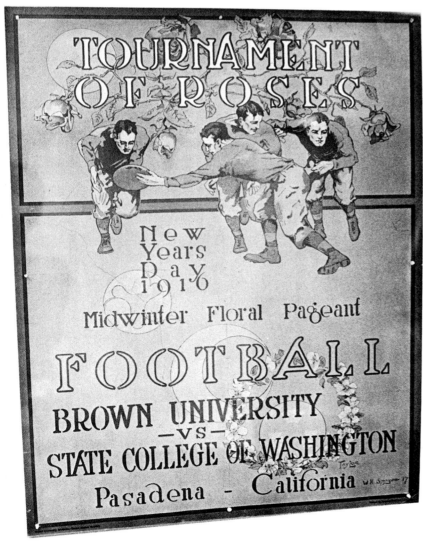

The new groups quickly made up for a relatively late start by fielding first-rate teams: the Washington Huskie teams under coach Gilmour "Gloomy Gil" Dobie were dominant on the West Coast, and Texas A & M, under head coach Dana Xenophon Bible, began a decade-long dynasty around 1917.

For many years, of course, football teams played mostly in their own "neighborhoods." Geography and economy dictated short distances for games, since group travel was by train. Also, the new organizations held conference championships, so that there was a goal to strive for every year, since cross-country interconference play was limited to experimental exhibition-type games.

Even then, however, there were famous independents, many of them the same as today: Notre Dame, Syracuse, Pittsburgh, and of course Army and Navy. These independent football powers could, by mutual agreement, play teams across the country regardless of conference affiliation, and many sports historians believe that independent play, together with superior coaches and teams, allowed schools like Notre Dame, Army and Navy to attract nationwide followings. Even today, college football fans across the country who never attended those particular schools root for Notre Dame, and stay glued to the Army/Navy game.

In general, however, centralized competition within a geographical conference became common throughout most of the rest of the country. From this type of year-after-year competition has sprung most of the intense rivalries which have helped make college football what it is. By playing each other annually, teams formed consistent strategies, learned from each other, and upgraded the level of play of the entire conference. Coaches looked forward to presenting rival coaches with a new play or formation and perhaps evening old scores.

Schools became known for certain styles of play, and in fact whole conferences developed offensive and defensive patterns – for instance, the Southwest Conference became the very heart of razzle-dazzle passing plays in the 1920s and continued in that vein for decades, whereas, until quite recently, Big Ten coaches have favored grind-it-out ground rushing and stalwart defense.

College football was developing as many styles of play as there were regional accents across America. True, football's best were streaming across the Atlantic to fight a world war, and some schools were putting football programs on hold while others played only informally. But, in reality, the war years were only a short breather before the charged-up season of 1919, when the boys came marching home for the Golden Decade of college football.

57

ABOVE: *Douglas "Peahead" Walker was Wake Forest's football coach from 1936 through 1950 – the last coach of the Demon Deacons to post a winning career record.*

BELOW: *Perhaps the most famous of all Pitt coaches was the legendary Jock Sutherland, who compiled a 107-20-7 record at Pitt from 1924 to 1938. Here he is shown with All-America halfback Marshall "Biggie" Goldberg, around 1937.*

ABOVE RIGHT: *Wallace "Wally" Wade began the process of turning Alabama into a twentieth-century powerhouse. He coached the Crimson Tide from 1923 to 1930 before heading to Duke, where he coached off and on from 1931 to 1950.*

RIGHT: *George Sauer, shown here with Navy quarterbacks Reaves Baysinger and Bob Horne in the spring of 1948, was the first civilian to coach the Midshipmen.*

OPPOSITE: *Chris "Red" Cagle (left) was a standout runner for Army, and a consensus All-American from 1926 through 1929. He is shown here with "Biff" Jones.*

The Galloping Ghost: Red Grange

It is hard to think of a less likely duo for football stardom than Bob Zuppke and Harold "Red" Grange. One was a short, German immigrant with a thick accent and a yearning to become a painter. The other was a Wheaton schoolboy who delivered ice to supplement his family's income.

But fate, in the form of Illini football, was to thrust the two together. Grange would drive Zuppke's 1923-25 Illinois teams to glory, and Zuppke would help make Grange immortal.

Bob Zuppke was a 5ft 7in philosophy major at the University of Wisconsin who dreamed of a career in commercial art. After graduation he taught art at Hackley Manual Training School in Muskegon, Michigan, where he also became the school's football coach. It soon became apparent that this diminutive German, who had never played varsity football for reasons which were all too obvious, was a coaching genius.

High school coaching in the Midwest, including at Oak Park High School in the Chicago area, inevitably led to his recruitment, in 1913, by University of Illinois athletic director George Huff. The following season, "Zup," as he was affectionately called, coached the Illini to the national title. In his 30 years as Illini coach, he won or shared seven Big Ten titles, managed four unbeaten teams and snagged three national championships. But coaching "The Wheaton Iceman" was his lasting claim to fame.

Harold Grange grew up in Wheaton, Illinois, and had played some football at Wheaton High School – along with other sports such as basketball, baseball and track. To his natural physique (he stood 5ft 10in and weighed 170 pounds) were added hard-won muscles from delivering ice from a horse-drawn wagon for extra money. He had won the job as a 14-year-old by hoisting a 100-pound block of ice onto his shoulder. Later, when he had become a living legend at Illinois, this romantic story spread, and pictures of "The Wheaton Iceman" with a cake of ice on his shoulder appeared in newspapers all over the country.

Red-haired "Red" Grange almost didn't play football for Illinois. After meeting with Coach Zuppke, who characteristically didn't offer more than token encouragement, Grange chose to attend Illinois but arrived in Champaign in 1922 intending to stick to basketball and track. But his new Zeta Psi fraternity brothers had other ideas. The athletic freshman was ordered to go out for football or face that dreaded fraternity punishment – a paddling.

Off he trudged to the football field. Grange reportedly took one look at the competition and returned to his fraternity house, convinced that he would not be good enough to play for Illinois. But the young giant was back the next day, possibly with a sore rear end, and within a week donned Illini uniform number 77. There must have been thunder in the heavens.

Grange made his varsity debut as a sophomore against Nebraska in 1923, romping for 208 yards against the stunned Cornhuskers and scoring every touchdown in that 24-7 victory. By the end of that fairy-tale season he had garnered 12 touchdowns in seven games, and led the nation in yardage gained with 1260.

The Illini were unbeaten, and more than that, they were on the map. Walter Camp himself threw aside his eastern bias and named Grange to his 1923 All-America list, along with Illini guard Jim McMillen. The hearts of Illini fans across the state beat faster, and everyone anticipated the fall of 1924, when the new Memorial Stadium would be dedicated before the game against rival Michigan – also unbeaten in 1923.

Grantland Rice had observed Grange as well, and sat down at his typewriter to describe the player he had seen. He wrote:

A streak of fire, a breath of flame,
Eluding all who reach and clutch;
A gray ghost thrown into the game
That rival hands may never touch;
A rubber bounding, blasting soul
Whose destination is the goal –
Red Grange of Illinois!

Of course, the nickname "Galloping Ghost" spread like prairie flames. Those were heady days for sports fans. Grange was the contemporary of larger-than-life characters like Babe Ruth, Bobby Jones, and Jack Dempsey. Over in Indiana, the Notre Dame backfield – also

OPPOSITE LEFT: *Diminutive coach Bob Zuppke of Illinois would become famous as Red Grange's mentor.*

OPPOSITE RIGHT: *Harold "Red" Grange, the most famous football player of his day, drew thousands to his college and professional games.*

TOP RIGHT: *Grange decked out in raccoon coat and hat, circa 1924.*

RIGHT: *Illinois' famous football duo: Grange and Coach Zuppke. Zuppke had never played football himself, but most acknowledge him as a coaching genius.*

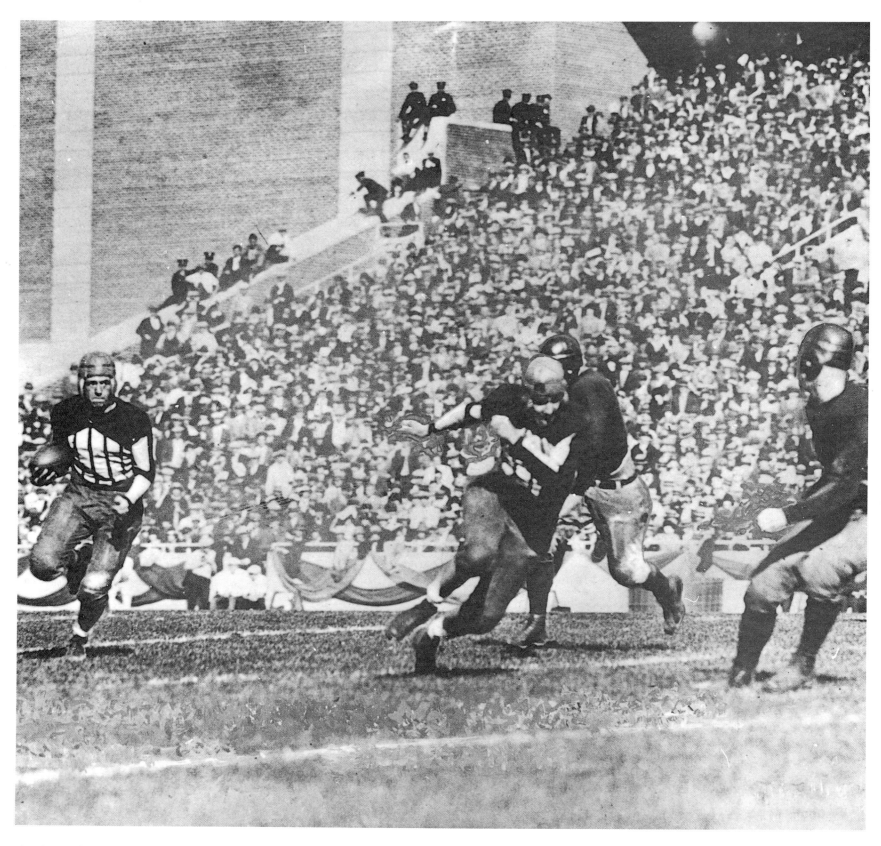

thanks to Grantland Rice – had been dubbed "The Four Horsemen," referring to the Apocalypse. Yet the Midwest, and the nation, yearned to idolize one single player, and this shy, red-haired magician was just the man.

As Grange returned to the Champaign campus for his junior year in the fall of 1924, anticipation was at fever pitch. The day approached for the Illinois-Michigan game, and no one could remember a more eagerly-awaited Illinois football game. Fraternity and sorority houses were decorated, fans streamed in by the thousands from Chicago, and legend has it that even the pennant races were temporarily forgotten.

It must be noted that between Bob Zuppke and Fielding Yost of Michigan, no love was lost. Zup had written to each Illini player several times over that summer, telling them how easily the Wolverines and Yost expected to win. Grange, like the others, had been taken in by Zuppke's propaganda, and years later he recalled:

Zup had worked on that game from the start of the summer. He started telling us all kinds of things Yost had been saying about us all summer. It wasn't until a long time afterward that I found out that Yost had been in Europe the whole summer.

The day of the Big Game, 18 October 1924, was clear and unseasonably warm, and Zuppke hit upon a last-minute piece of psychological warfare. He ordered his players, over their protests, to remove their heavy woollen stockings, which all footballers wore on their lower legs in those days.

When the Illini took the field, Yost immediately noticed their bare legs and ran over to make sure that no lubrication had been applied to their legs. As the teams made ready for the opening kickoff, the temperature was already soaring past 80 degrees, and suddenly the Michigan players began to feel rather warm and weighed down by their wool stockings. But they should have been worrying about Red Grange.

In the first 12 minutes of the game, Red Grange ran for four touchdowns. He scored them on runs of 95, 67, 56 and 44 yards. Zuppke, realizing that his star, bare-legged or no, was exhausted, sat Grange down on the bench to rest. The din from the Memorial Stadium's first crowd was unlike anything ever heard. One witness described it as "something not heard since Caesar's return to Rome in triumph from the Wars."

Zuppke kept Grange out of the game until the second half, when he was sent in to score his fifth touchdown, then pass to Marion Leonard

Although Grange had become a Midwestern sensation, it wasn't until the 1925 season, when Grange singlehandedly destroyed Penn, that eastern heads were bowed to him as well.

Though the Penn field was deep in mud from recent downpours, Grange rushed for 363 yards that day, scoring three touchdowns on runs of 56, 13 and 20 yards. Illinois won 24-2 as Lawrence Stallings, up in the Penn press box, tried to write a color story on the game. The ex-Marine, who had written *What Price Glory*, struggled at his typewriter for an hour before tearing up what he had written. "I can't write it," he sighed. "It's too big."

At the end of the season, even as Grange was being named All-America again, it was announced that the Galloping Ghost was turning professional. He had signed a contract with another Illinois alum – George Halas – to play with the Chicago Bears. The stingy Halas had signed Grange to the richest contract in the league's young history. Zuppke reportedly had tried to dissuade young Grange from leaving school, but without success.

In his Illinois career, Grange had compiled a record of 3637 yards rushing, and another 643 passing – in only 20 games over three years.

Paul Sann, in his book *The Lawless Decade*, described the impact of a player like Red Grange on the fast-living generation of the Roaring Twenties:

Red Grange, number 77, made Jack Dempsey move over. He put college football ahead of boxing as the Golden Age picked up momentum. He also made some of the ball yards obsolete. They couldn't handle the crowds. He made people buy more radios. How could you wait until Sunday morning to find out what deeds Red Grange had performed on Saturday? He was 'The Galloping Ghost', and he made sports historians torture their portables without mercy.

So the little German and the Wheaton red-head went their separate ways – Grange to the pros with the Chicago Bears, and Zuppke on to more great seasons, notably 1927 and 1928, coaching the Illini.

But Zuppke, who tried never to have favorites among his players, had lost his heart to Grange, or "Grench," as he pronounced it. "I will never have another Grange," he said at the time, "but neither will anyone else. They can argue all they like about the greatest player that ever lived. I'm satisfied I had him when I had Grange."

for Illinois' sixth – and mercifully final – touchdown. The Wolverines stood looking at the scoreboard in disbelief as time wound down. They had lost 39-14.

Illinois went on to a second-place tie in the Big Ten, but Grange was again voted All-America, and added to it the *Chicago Tribune*'s first Big Ten MVP award.

OPPOSITE: *The "Galloping Ghost" in action. Opposing defenders learned to dread his runs, such as this one during the famous Illinois-Michigan game of 1924. Grange scored four times in the first 12 minutes of the game.*

TOP: *Grange gazes down at his number 77 Illinois jersey for the last time. He turned professional after the 1925 season.*

RIGHT: *Red Grange signs a contract to play professional football with the Chicago Bears, as owners C.C. Pyle (left) and Illinois alumnus George Halas look on.*

The Four Horsemen and The Rock

The decade of the Roaring Twenties is often referred to as the "golden decade" of college football. Certainly football enjoyed an unprecedented boom with the return of the soldiers from Europe, who gladly threw off their military uniforms and donned leather helmets.

With the boom in football came marching bands, the crowds and the money – for the nation was football-mad, and enormous crowds gathered to watch the "big-draw" teams. These included Army, Navy, Illinois, Michigan, California – and Notre Dame.

Notre Dame was the Camelot of college football in the Golden Twenties, and head football coach Knute Rockne, called "The Swede" or "The Rock," was King Arthur. His legend as a coach, mentor and motivator of men has indeed approached Arthurian proportions. He coached the Gipper and the Four Horsemen, but he was more famous than any of them, and countless sportswriters have added to that fame.

McCallum and Pearson's *College Football USA 1869-1972* describes Rockne's place in the football world of the 1920s:

And dominating the scene was the little man with the crinkled nose, the bright eyes and the crisp, staccato manner of talking – on the radio, in the newspapers, in the movies, on the field – Rockne, of Notre Dame. Schools received publicity either because they used the Rockne system or because they didn't. Graduates from his teams dotted the country in coaching positions, spreading his gospel. A coincidence – a football-mad nation, postwar, halcyon days, money days – and Knute Rockne.

From 1920 to 1930, his Irish teams lost but 11 games while winning 93. Unlike Michigan's Juggernaut, they ranged from coast to coast, flinging their passes into the damp air of the Atlantic Seaboard or the clear blue of the Pacific Slope. They made Pittsburgh and Atlanta and Philadelphia their way stations, looked in on Baltimore, and New York with its 'subway alumni' was their second home.

And always out in front of them, guiding, shouting, encouraging, leaving his indelible imprint – Rockne.

Perhaps it was, as McCallum and Pearson have suggested, partially that Notre Dame remained independent and therefore acquired a national reputation more easily. They didn't just beat their conference rivals – they thrashed everybody. But there is no doubt that Rockne's

ABOVE: *All-America halfback George "The Gipper" Gipp of Notre Dame.*

LEFT: *Actor Ronald Reagan in his role as George Gipp in the Hollywood film* Knute Rockne – All-American *(1940).*

OPPOSITE: *Perhaps the most famous college football coach of all time, Knute Rockne. As coach of the Notre Dame Fighting Irish, Rockne had a profound influence on the mass popularity of college football.*

coaching prowess, skill and motivational techniques helped make Notre Dame the most talked-about, most admired and most imitated of college teams.

Rockne knew how to talk to sportswriters – in fact, today's college coaches could take a lesson from him. He always had a colorful quote or anecdote ready. The apocryphal story about George Gipp's deathbed request to Rockne to implore his Irish players to "win one for the Gipper," immortalized by Pat O'Brien and Ronald Reagan in the movie *Knute Rockne – All American* (1940), was reportedly first told to Grantland Rice by Rockne the night before the 1928 Army game, in which the Cadets were favored.

ABOVE: *Halfback "Sleepy Jim" Crowley heads downfield. As one of the famous Four Horsemen of the 1924 Notre Dame backfield, Crowley achieved fame as a great broken-field runner and nimble wit. He carried the ball 1932 yards in three varsity years.*

RIGHT: *The most famous publicity photo ever taken of college football players was this of the Four Horsemen, in uniform and on horseback. From left to right: Don Miller, Elmer Layden, Jim Crowley, and Harry Stuhldreher.*

"Grant, I've never asked the boys to pull one out for Gipp. Tomorrow I might have to," Rockne predicted. The next day, the halftime score was 0-0, and Rockne decided to play his trump card. The rest is history, of course, and Rice watched with the rest of the crowd as the inspired Irish (some say the players were sobbing as they took the field for the fourth quarter) won, 12-6. "I knew they were playing with a 12th man – George Gipp," Rice later recalled.

The story of the backfield quartet known as The Four Horsemen began, of course, with the recruitment of Don Miller, Elmer Layden, Harry Stuhldreher and "Sleepy Jim" Crowley to play for Notre Dame. While none of the four were standouts as freshmen, each had vastly improved as they had played together, and each had a unique talent and personality.

Stuhldreher was a leader on the field, Rockne later remembered, and was also "a good and fearless blocker." Fleet, quiet Layden had an uncanny knack for intercepting passes. "Sleepy Jim" Crowley, who "always resembled a lad about to get out of or into bed," became as famous for his wit and conversation as for his outstanding broken-field running. And Don Miller surprised Rockne with "his fleetness and daring . . . a halfback to cheer the heart of any coach."

On 18 October 1924, the Irish were on their way to a national championship and were playing the annual test against Army. The backfield of four rather small young men (Layden was the largest, at 6ft and 162 pounds) did themselves and Rockne proud that day, scoring two touchdowns and prompting Grantland Rice to immortalize them in the following day's *New York Herald Tribune*:

Outlined against a blue-gray October sky, The Four Horsemen rode again. In dramatic lore they are known as famine, pestilence, destruction and death. These are only aliases. Their real names are: Stuhldreher, Miller, Crowley and Layden. They formed the crest of the South Bend cyclone before which another fighting Army team was swept over the precipice at the Polo Grounds this afternoon, as 55,000 spectators peered down upon the bewildered panorama spread out upon the green plain below.

LEFT: *Stanford's star fullback Ernie Nevers faced the Four Horsemen and Notre Dame in the 1925 Rose Bowl – and lost.*

OPPOSITE TOP: *The 1925 Rose Bowl: Stuhldreher of Notre Dame intercepts a Stanford pass. The Irish won 27-10.*

OPPOSITE BOTTOM: *Irish coach Knute Rockne knew how to motivate his players without breaking their spirits. He was universally loved by players and fans alike. Shown here in 1930, he would die in a plane crash the following year.*

This tribute from the leading sportswriter of the day prompted Rockne's alert young publicity aide, George Strickler (who would later become the *Chicago Tribune*'s sports editor) to have the four backs photographed, in uniform, on four old plow horses he had found on the Notre Dame farm. Wire services were quick to pick up the photo and the Rice quote, and soon the four quiet men were the talk of the nation.

Notre Dame went on to the national championship, and demolished Stanford in the Rose Bowl. Three of the Four Horsemen were All-America that year, and Miller, it was said, lost out to Red Grange. So famous were the four that 25 years later they were reunited on horseback, as smiling middle-aged men. All went on to illustrious coaching, executive or judicial careers.

Such were the fortunes of Notre Dame while Rockne reigned. It wasn't all sweetness and victories, however. When the Irish lost, Rockne could rave, break things and call down the heavens to mock his players. He was a master of dripping sarcasm. "Sorry," he would say, sticking his head in the door at halftime, when they were losing, "I thought this was the Fighting Irish locker room!" Another afternoon, after a lackluster first half, Rockne mocked his players, "Remember,

girls, let's not have any rough stuff out there."

But somehow, instead of breaking the spirit of his players, Rockne inspired them to incredible feats. Rockne was never false, and that is why he earned the undying devotion of his friends, players, writers, and the man in the street. He believed in Notre Dame and the Fighting Irish to the last breath – and he made others believe in them too. "Rockne sold football to the men on the trolley, the elevated, the subway," explained pupil Harry Mehre, later head coach at Georgia. "He sold it to the baker, the butcher, the pipefitter who never went to college. He made it an American mania."

Rockne died in a plane crash in Kansas in 1931, and the nation mourned. His last Fighting Irish team carried him to his grave, near the campus under a giant oak.

And it is said, in South Bend, where many famous coaches and players have earned glory for Notre Dame in the years since, that the locker room still echoes Knute Rockne's pre-game chants, the ones that sent the Fighting Irish screaming out the door to another victory: "Go out there and hit 'em! Crack 'em! Fight to live! Fight to win! Fight to win, win, win, WIN!"

Poets in the Press Box

Coach Bob Zuppke of Illinois once remarked, "Often an All-American is made by a long run, a weak defense, and a poet in the press box." Certainly the caliber of men who reported on football in those days deserve a measure of the credit for turning it into a national passion.

Great writers who just happened to cover sports in the first half of the century included Paul Gallico, Damon Runyon, Ring Lardner and Westbrook Pegler. These men wrote about sports as part of American culture, just as they wrote about politics, government and the arts. Social commentary from the press box at a football game came naturally to them.

The dean of them all, undoubtedly, was Grantland Rice. He named the Four Horsemen and the Galloping Ghost. For more than 50 years, from 1901 through most of 1954, he turned out some 67,000,000 words – 22,000 newspaper columns, 7000 sets of verse and over 1000 magazine articles. He was also a broadcaster. At the age of 73, Rice was still writing a famous syndicated column six days a week for 80 papers throughout the country.

and larger-than-life aura of college football in print – to the vast delight of millions of people.

Grantland Rice died at his typewriter in July of 1954, and American football had lost a friend. Perhaps his most famous lines were the ending of his verse *Alumnus Football*, and they epitomized his seamless meshing of sport and life: "For when the One Great Scorer comes to mark against your name, He writes – not that you won or lost – but how you played the Game."

OPPOSITE: *The dean of American sportswriters: Grantland Rice, circa 1925.*

ABOVE: *Writer Paul Gallico.*

TOP RIGHT: *Author Damon Runyon also wrote about sports.*

RIGHT: *Ring Lardner in 1925.*

Rice wielded enormous power through his ability to immortalize players, coaches and teams in print for the millions who hadn't watched the game themselves – but he was by all accounts a modest man. "I owe sport a great deal," he would often say, although his friends felt it was the other way around.

In a field that was jealously competitive, everyone loved Grantland Rice. He was generous with advice and assistance, and there was hardly a sports hack in the land who hadn't learned something from Granny. There was only one problem. No one could write the way he did – romantically, dramatically, calling in references to ancient lore – but the imitations were so bad that they gave sportswriting a bad name in some circles.

He was the perfect chronicler of the times, because Americans wanted to believe that football players were immortal gods, that coaches were all-wise and all-knowing, and that their favorite team had as its heavenly mission to subdue the forces of darkness and emerge victorious. Rice never neglected the facts, but he caught the drama

Giants of the Midwest

No less an authority on toughness than General William T Sherman remarked in his memoirs of the Civil War that although the Confederates had usually been more than a match for the eastern Union soldiers on the battlefields, it had been the farm boys of the Midwest that had outfought, outlasted and just plain broken the backs of the Confederacy. "Our cornbelt pioneers had not forgotten how to use their legs," Sherman ruefully admitted. "They could really march."

And they still can. College football in the Midwest has taken root like the crops themselves, and like the crops, no matter how much is harvested, there is always more springing up to take its place. From the two major conferences, the Big Ten and Big Eight, to its major independents, football Midwestern-style has been in the spotlight more often than not.

The first half of this century was a particularly fertile one, so to speak. Here are some Midwesterners, of all sizes, who became giants on the football field.

Walter Eckersall weighed all of 138 pounds when he enrolled at the University of Chicago in 1903. He was a cool-as-a-cucumber quarterback who could run like lightning and kick with awesome precision. Eckersall stood out on Amos Alonzo Stagg's Chicago teams of 1904-06, and he makes most historians' all-time teams for the first half of the century.

Knute Rockne later recalled seeing Eckersall as a high-school player in a championship game, and credited his play with giving him a keen interest in football. "Eckersall's sharp, staccato calling of signals, his keen, handsome face, and the smooth precision with which he drove and countered and drove again, handling his players with the rhythm of an orchestra leader – all this gave football a new meaning to me." As the captain of the Fighting Irish many years later, Rockne finally got to shake Eckersall's hand – his hero was referee that day as Notre Dame played Chicago. As Rockne waxed poetic about what Eckersall had meant to him, Walter said, "Stop, stop – or Notre Dame will be penalized five yards for speechmaking!"

Bronislaw "Bronko" Nagurski makes the all-century team as a true Midwestern giant. He was a fullback and tackle for Minnesota in the 1920s, and even played end once or twice. Considered enormous in those days at 6ft 2in and 217 pounds, Nagurski was fearless, inspired, and, goes the legend, numb to physical pain. A mild-mannered Minnesota son of the prairie, he went on to stardom as a fullback for the Chicago Bears. "There has probably never been a football player any stronger than Nagurski," recalled Pudge Heffelfinger, "or any who could develop so much horsepower from a standing start."

Nagurski, whose teammates unabashedly marvelled at his physical strength, often explained that he owed his muscular power to plowing. "But every farmer's son has done plowing," someone pointed out to him. "Yes, but not without horses!" Bronko would laugh.

Charles "Chic" Harley may have been the man who made the state of Ohio the nation's football mecca, circa 1919. The triple-threat wonder helped give the Ohio State Buckeyes their first victory over archrival Michigan, and he is said to have wept in frustration when the Illini, with Red Grange, handed him his only defeat as a Buckeye, with a last-second field goal.

OPPOSITE: *This 1930 annual meeting of the Big Ten Conference brought together some of the leading voices of college football, including A.A. Stagg, Fritz Crisler, Fielding Yost and Kenneth Wilson.*

ABOVE: *Walter Eckersall: The pint-size quarterback was cool as a cucumber for Chicago in 1904-06.*

TOP RIGHT: *Amiable giant Bronko Nagurski of Minnesota football fame had legendary strength.*

Slight of build, good-natured and a little shy, Harley could run, pass and kick with the best of them, but perhaps his quick thinking and daring were his most brilliant traits. Once, in a game against Wisconsin, Harley grabbed the ball from a Badger runner who was in hot pursuit of a touchdown, and dashed for the opposite goal without breaking stride. Walter Camp picked him for three All-America teams in the years straddling World War I, and called him "one of the greatest players the country has ever seen."

Jay Berwanger was a big blond Iowan who had brought the University of Chicago its first All-America certificate in 11 years in 1934. A halfback whose rough-and-tough physique and fighting instinct earned him distinction, he was also a crack kicker. In 1936 Berwanger participated in one of the very first College All-Star games, which at that time were played against professional teams. He later became a well-known college football referee.

Thomas D Harmon was the god of Wolverine football in the years just before World War II, and is always mentioned with the most famous college players of all time. His stats are amazing even by Michigan standards – and along with trusty quarterback Forrest Evashevski, he brought the magic back to a program which had been in a slump.

In Tom Harmon's three years at Ann Arbor, he carried the ball 398 times for 2338 yards (just under six yards per try); completed 101 of

233 passes for 16 touchdowns; and scored 237 points on 33 touchdowns, points-after and field goals. He led the nation in both passing and running in 1939 and 1940, rewriting Red Grange's Big Ten records as he took Heisman honors in his senior year and was also awarded Associated Press Athlete-of-the-Year.

Harmon and Grange were often compared when the question of all-time backs came up, and Amos Alonzo Stagg, for one, voted in favor of Harmon. "Harmon was superior to Grange in everything but running," he claimed. "I'll take Harmon on my team and you can have all the rest."

Harmon's post-college career was similarly illustrious. Enlisting in the Air Force in World War II, the young man was forced to bail out of planes twice, and was given up for dead – once making it back to an American base in China after a month of hiding from the Japanese. He returned home a hero, sporting a Silver Star, Purple Heart and burned legs. Nevertheless, he returned to the gridiron as a professional with the Los Angeles Rams, married movie actress Elyse Knox, and became a successful network sportscaster. One of the Harmon's three children is TV and film star Mark Harmon.

Midwesterners think they have a lock on football toughness, but in the years just before World War II other regional powerhouses were vying for public attention – and promoting new bowl games.

LEFT: *Charles W. "Chic" Harley of Ohio State helped popularize football in Ohio.*

ABOVE: *Jay Berwanger of Chicago, plunging for yards against Wisconsin, 1934. He was the first Heisman Trophy winner.*

RIGHT: *Tom Harmon was perhaps the greatest Wolverine ever. All-American in 1939 and 1940, he won the Heisman in 1940.*

OPPOSITE TOP RIGHT: *Harmon (right) with favorite blocker Forrest Evashevski in 1940.*

Orange, Sugar, Cotton: New Bowl Games

The Rose Bowl had had a rather rough beginning in 1902 – Michigan annihilated Stanford and the game was prematurely called – but since the resumption of the football game finale of the Tournament of Roses in 1916 (Brown vs Washington State), the event had become an institution.

Many illustrious games had been played – Notre Dame's Four Horsemen versus Stanford in 1925, Alabama and Johnny Mack Brown against the Washington Huskies and George "Wildcat" Wilson in 1926, and the Crimson Tide again, this time with Dixie Howell and Paul Bryant, against Stanford in 1935.

By the late 1920s Rose Bowl games were drawing 60,000 fans or more. Other regions with pleasant winter weather and no shortage of raving football fans began dreaming of having their own bowl games. Bowl game advocates saw the advantage of hosting a major sporting event and thus drawing positive publicity to their city, pleasing their local football fans – and no doubt making some money as well.

In 1933 a group of businessmen and civic officials in balmy, tourist-happy Miami inaugurated the Palm Festival. The idea was to pit the University of Miami, which was a relative infant in the world of college athletics, against whatever respectable team would agree to come down to play them.

Some 3500 fans showed up for the first game, played on 2 January, which featured New York's Manhattan College as the designated opponent. Manhattan had been favored but was held scoreless by Miami, which won 7-0. The next year, however, Duquesne made the trip and demolished the Hurricanes 33-7.

In 1935, the name of the event was changed to the Orange Bowl Festival, and a new charter was drawn up. The first official Orange Bowl game was played where the Orange Bowl Stadium now stands, in what was then a small wooden-bleachered field which held 5000 people.

Since then, the annual Orange Bowl game has been a mighty challenge to some of football's best, and has proven to be unpredictable and entertaining. Favorites don't always fare well in the Orange Bowl. Joe Namath's Crimson Tide team found that out in 1965 when an inspired Texas Longhorn defense turned away their rally to win 21-17. Nebraska learned it the hard way in 1984 when they were edged out 31-30 by the Miami Hurricanes and Bernie Kosar. The Orange Bowl of 1975 was Ara Parseghian's last game as head coach of Notre Dame, and the Irish won it for him, 13-11, against a Bear Bryant Alabama team which had been ranked Number 1 in the nation.

OPPOSITE TOP: *The Tournament of Roses Parade: An annual ritual before the Rose Bowl football game.*

OPPOSITE BOTTOM: *The Orange Bowl started in Miami in 1934 and has been among the greatest New Year's Day contests ever since.*

ABOVE: *An aerial view of the Rose Bowl in Pasadena, California.*

LEFT: *Oklahoma Sooners Tony Casillas and Jeff Tupper hold the Orange Bowl Trophy after defeating the Penn State Nittany Lions in the 1986 Orange Bowl.*

ABOVE: *The Georgia Bulldogs take the field at the 1983 Sugar Bowl.*

RIGHT: *Tulane's Sugar Bowl Stadium holds 73,000 fans.*

BOTTOM: *The Sugar Bowl trophy.*

The Sugar Bowl was the dream of the publisher of the *New Orleans Item*, Colonel James M Thompson, and his sports columnist Fred Digby. From its inception in 1927 it took almost eight years for the first Sugar Bowl game to be played, on 1 January 1935. Digby dreamed of a winter sports carnival, with a variety of athletic competitions, highlighted by the football game. Different political and city factions within New Orleans, however, did not immediately jump on the Digby bandwagon. It was Digby's steadfast faith in his idea which finally rallied enough support to stage the first Sugar Bowl game in Tulane Stadium in 1935.

To name the game the Sugar Bowl seemed natural to Digby because Louisiana was at the time the nation's leading sugar producer, and because Tulane Stadium had been built on the site of a former sugar plantation.

There have been some great Sugar Bowl games. In 1945, Alabama's freshman quarterback Harry Gilmer gave an early indication of his star promise although the Crimson Tide lost to the Duke Blue Devils and star fullback Tom Davis, 29-26. The 1947 Sugar Bowl was billed as the battle of the All-America halfbacks, pitting Georgia's Charley Trippi and North Carolina's aptly-named Charlie "Choo Choo" Justice, in a contest which the Georgia Bulldogs won 20-10.

The 1951 event pitted Bud Wilkinson's Oklahoma juggernaut, with a winning streak of 31 games, against Bear Bryant's Kentucky team, which beat the Sooners 13-7 on a fourth-quarter touchdown. And the 1979 Sugar Bowl saw the Number 2 Crimson Tide of Alabama, where Bryant now practiced his magic, defeat Joe Paterno's Number-1-ranked Penn State Nittany Lions 14-7. Paterno avenged this bitter loss, which denied Penn State the national championship, in 1983 by beating Georgia and Herschel Walker 27-23 with top running back Curt Warner, for the national prize.

The Sugar Bowl certainly has the most distinguished trophy of any post-season bowl game – a rare and priceless sterling silver bowl made in England in 1830, purchased by prominent New Orleans antique dealer Samuel Waldhorn on a European trip. Sugar Bowl organizers made a passionate appeal to Waldhorn's civic pride to obtain the gorgeous piece for the winner of the game. The winner receives the trophy for one year, and then a replica is donated for the team's permanent possession.

The first Cotton Bowl took place in Dallas in 1937, showcasing Texas Christian's brilliant Sammy Baugh in his last college game. Texas oil magnate J Curtis Sanford had seen the Rose Bowl and had heard about the imminent start-ups of the Orange and Sugar Bowls. Why not one in his hometown?

Not an immediate success from an attendance standpoint (only 17,000 saw the first game), the Cotton Bowl limped along as something of an also-ran postseason contest until the newly-formed Cotton Bowl Athletic Association was instituted as an agency of the Southwest Conference in 1940. Two years later, it was announced that the winner of that illustrious football conference would automatically be invited to play in the Cotton Bowl.

The Cotton Bowl has, ever since, provided the nation with a glimpse of the glories of Southwest Conference football, and there have been many memorable games. The 1949 contest saw Southern Methodist's Doak Walker and Kyle Rote defeat Oregon and its star quarterback

Norm Van Brocklin, 21-13. In 1957, Texas Christian beat Syracuse and its brilliant All-American Jim Brown, 28-27.

The 1970 Cotton Bowl pitted Ara Parseghian's Notre Dame, in its first bowl game in 45 years, against Number-1-ranked Texas under coach Darrell Royal. Notre Dame's quarterback that year was Joe Theismann, and the Longhorns were favored only by seven points – even with former President Lyndon B Johnson in the stands rooting for them. As it was, Texas pulled out the game 21-17 on a series of fourth-down gambles.

The Cotton Bowl of 1983 was a true battle of All-Americans (and future NFL superstars) as the SMU Mustangs, sporting tailback Eric Dickerson, faced the Pitt Panthers with trusty quarterback Dan Marino. Southern Methodist took the game 7-3 in an unexpected defensive show.

The effort of civic leaders and sports-minded boosters to fund, promote and organize successful Bowl classics cannot be underestimated, since throughout the first part of the century many bowls were conceived of, then dead a few years later. Many suffered from poor management by well-meaning but incompetent organizers. Others may have been scams. Who remembers the Camellia Bowl of 1948? Or the Oil Bowls of 1946 and 1947? Or the Bacardi Bowl in Havana, Cuba in 1937, pitting Auburn against Villanova?

Even as the organizers of the new bowl games were savoring their successes, there was war brewing in Europe. What would it mean for college football?

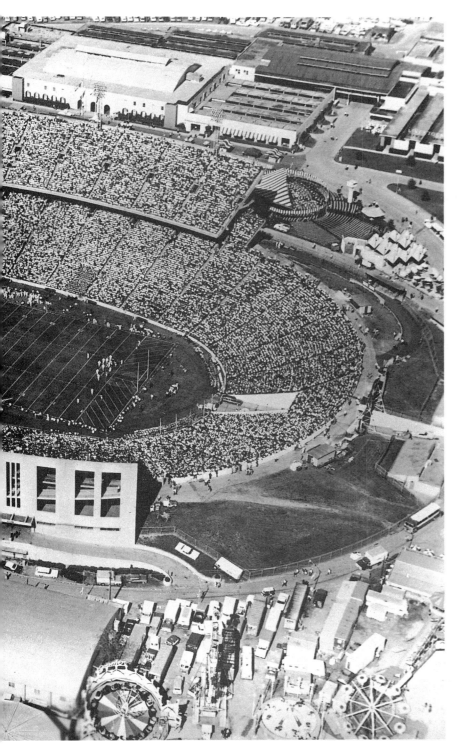

OPPOSITE BOTTOM LEFT: *TCU's sensational Sammy Baugh inaugurated the Cotton Bowl in his last college game, in 1937.*

LEFT: *The Cotton Bowl, site of the annual Texas ritual. Some memorable games have been played here.*

ABOVE: *Notre Dame coach Ara Parseghian counsels Irish quarterback Joe Theismann during Notre Dame's 24-11 victory over Texas in the 1971 Cotton Bowl.*

BELOW: *Texas had beaten Notre Dame in the 1970 Cotton Bowl, 21-17. Here, the Longhorns take it over for a touchdown.*

PART III

The Dynasty Years: 1941-1982

The War Years

Just as World War II was finally enveloping the United States with the Japanese attack on Pearl Harbor, college football was turning an important corner with a successful new formation, and with a rules change. Maryland and Pennsylvania had met on 5 October 1940 for the first televised football game, and more new Bowl games were inaugurated – the Gator Bowl in 1946 in Jacksonville, Florida, and the Tangerine Bowl in 1947 in Orlando.

Coach Bernie Bierman's Minnesota teams had won conference championships in 1934, 1935, 1937 and 1938 – with his 1934 and 1936 teams ranked Number 1 in the country. He would coach two more national championship teams in 1940 and 1941 before going into the service. Great Golden Gopher players in those years included halfback Bruce Smith, who won the Heisman Trophy in 1941.

Stanley Woodward of the *New York Herald Tribune* made an astute observation on the 1941 team, and by implication the entire Big Ten, when he wrote, "Its forte is straightaway, undisguised power. It has tremendous men, and it advances the ball by using massed force against one point or the other of the line. . . . It is obvious that the pass does not hold a prominent position in Bierman's scheme. It is purely a last resort . . ."

PREVIOUS PAGE: *O.J. Simpson rides in triumph after USC beat UCLA 21-20 in 1967.*

TOP: *UCLA's Jackie Robinson in 1939. He went on to pro baseball fame with the Dodgers.*

ABOVE: *Yale's Larry Kelley garnered the 1936 Heisman.*

RIGHT: *Colorado's Byron "Whizzer" White: All-American in the late 1930s, Rhodes Scholar, later Supreme Court Justice.*

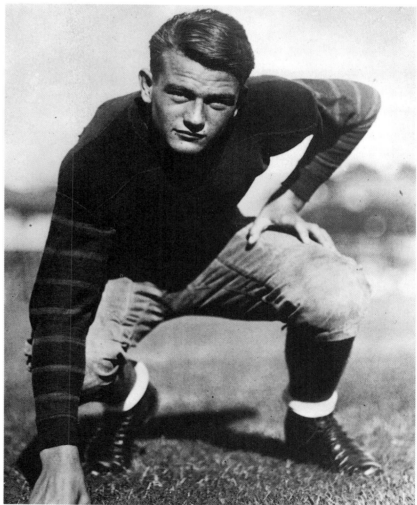

TOP: *Fordham's "Seven Blocks of Granite" of the 1930s. Vince Lombardi is third from left.*

LEFT: *Northwestern's Otto Graham was a 1943 Heisman runner-up.*

ABOVE: *John Wayne, as he looked during three years on the USC varsity. He was rated a top player by sports editors in the West.*

Also competitive in the Big Ten were Fritz Crisler's Wolverines of Michigan, featuring the sensational Tom Harmon. In 1940 the Wolverines led the conference in scoring, total offense, total defense, passing defense, percentage of pass completions and punting average. In 1954, Forrest Evashevski wrote of Crisler, "He was a stern taskmaster, a very lucid lecturer, and a very fine gentleman. In the three years that I played for Crisler, I never heard him use profanity or vulgarity and, while oftentimes he lost his patience, never did he lose his temper."

The "Cinderella" team for 1940 was the Stanford Indians under Clark Shaughnessy. Shaughnessy had been left without a team to coach at the end of the 1939 season after the University of Chicago dropped college football for good. In 1940 he led Stanford, which had lost all its conference games the year before, to an undefeated season which included a 21-13 victory over Nebraska in the Rose Bowl. Shaughnessy was voted Coach of the Year and his backfield of Frankie Albert, Pete Kmetovic, Hugh Gallarneau and Norman Standlee was praised across the land.

It was also a victory for the "T formation," which Shaughnessy, together with George Halas of the Chicago Bears, used to such thrilling advantage. The new style of play was arrived at by taking the original T, football's oldest formation, and putting a new spin on it by adding a "man in motion." Instead of a backfield shift into a box pattern with the backs shifting and the ends flexing, as demonstrated by Rockne's Notre Dame teams, only one man shifted – either right or left.

The combination of the T and the man in motion started a minor offensive revolution, allowing for a hard-hitting, quick-opening attack

OPPOSITE TOP LEFT: *Beattie Feathers was a standout halfback on the great 1931 Tennessee team.*

OPPOSITE TOP RIGHT: *Bernie Bierman, great coach of Minnesota in the mid-1930s.*

OPPOSITE BOTTOM: *Center Gerry Ford of the Michigan Wolverines, before his White House days.*

ABOVE: *Minnesota's National Champion 1934 Gophers, which included three All-Americans – Captain Pug Lund (front row, holding ball), Bill Bevan (front row, fourth from left), and Frank Larson (not shown).*

RIGHT: *Minnesota's Bruce Smith, an unstoppable halfback who nabbed the 1941 Heisman Trophy.*

and a high degree of offensive flexibility. Defenses were burdened with the wide variety of patterns an offense could employ. Even coaches who did not use the new scheme had to add new offensive features to stay competitive. Frank Leahy at Boston College, Clipper Smith at Villanova and Jim Crowley at Fordham did some streamlining of the "Notre Dame" style of offense. Leahy did finally adopt the new T when he was called to coach Notre Dame in 1941.

The year 1941 also saw a new rule allowing free substitution, and permitting substitutes to communicate immediately with teammates on the field. Therefore they could bring in plays from the sideline. This rule led, by the mid-1940s, to the introduction of "platoons" of offensive and defensive units. (In 1953 it was done away with and the clock turned back to 60-minute players – to howls of protest by coaches.)

ABOVE: *Tom Harmon and teammates with Wolverine coach Fritz Crisler, during the war years.*

RIGHT: *The Cinderella team of 1941, the Stanford Indians, with their great backfield – Hugh Gallarneau, Norm Standlee, Frankie Albert, and Pete Kmetovic.*

As 1942 progressed, the war hit home and many coaches and players enlisted and were sent overseas. Green freshmen got a chance to play football even at the best schools, as the ranks of available talent were thinned considerably. Dim-out regulations meant no more practice sessions under the lights, and gas rationing forced some games to be relocated. Game attendance dropped as a result, by approximately 19 percent.

Unnecessary travel was restricted during the war, and travel to college football games would be no exception. The practice of running railroad specials to sporting events was banned, and as a result the annual Army-Navy game was held in Annapolis for the first time since 1893. This edition of the game was played before fewer than 12,000 fans, rather than the enormous crowds of 100,000 or more that were common when the game was held in Philadelphia.

RIGHT: *Paul Christman, Missouri's All-American tailback, was part of the fine 1939 Tiger team.*

ABOVE: *Coach Clark Shaughnessy of Stanford was a successful innovator in the early 1940s.*

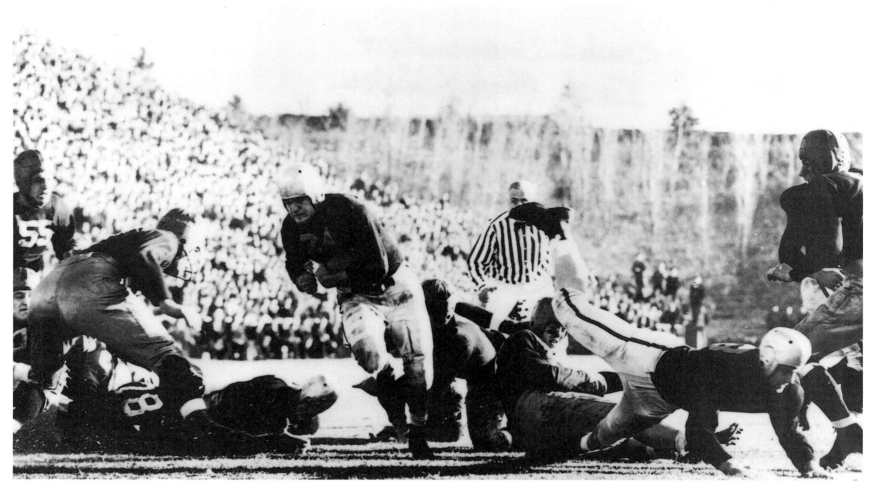

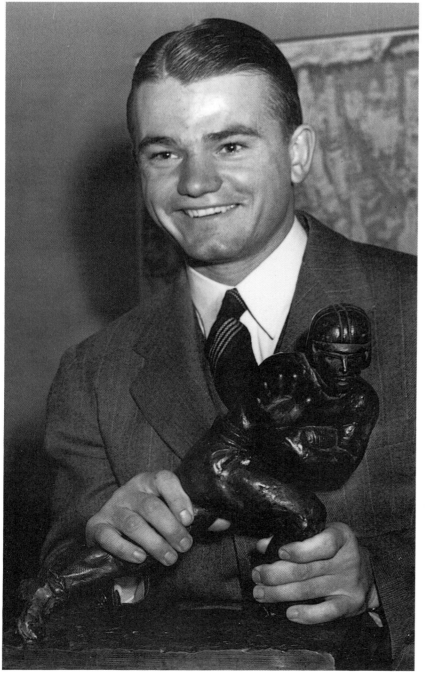

OPPOSITE TOP: *Iowa's Nile Kinnick, a slashing runner for the 1939 Hawkeyes.*

OPPOSITE LEFT: *Nile Kinnick with his 1939 Heisman Trophy. His acceptance speech is still quoted.*

OPPOSITE RIGHT: *Navy flier Kinnick, circa 1942. He was lost at sea in 1943.*

ABOVE: *The Notre Dame-Army contest of 1943 featured Irish fullback Creighton Miller.*

Yet, despite these restrictions and inconveniences, football carried on proudly. Army and Navy officers, in fact, stressed to President Franklin D Roosevelt the value of college football in training future military officers. Teamwork and leadership, they said, are not so very different in football as they are in combat.

Of course, there were great football players who never came back from the war. Iowa's brilliant halfback Nile Kinnick, the 1939 Heisman Trophy winner, was lost at sea in 1943, after having disappointed the ravenous professional football scouts by announcing his intention of attending law school after the service.

The University of Iowa's intelligent and articulate star, in accepting the 1939 Heisman, said, "I thank God that I was born to the gridirons of the Middle West and not to the battlefields of Europe. I can speak confidently and positively that the football players of this country would rather fight for the Heisman Trophy than for the Croix de Guerre."

A Place Called Notre Dame

As the 1940s progressed, the successors of Knute Rockne and George Gipp were proving that Notre Dame was no football fluke.

In 1943, Frank Leahy coached the Fighting Irish to a national championship behind Johnny Lujack and Angelo Bertelli. Lujack had large shoes to fill in taking over for Bertelli, who had quarterbacked the Irish from 1941 to midway through the 1943 season, when the young Italian six-footer left for Marine boot camp.

In Bertelli's three-year Notre Dame career, he completed 169 passes out of 324 thrown, for 2470 yards and 29 touchdowns. He was awarded the 1943 Heisman Trophy even though he hadn't completed the season, winning out over other outstanding candidates like Otto Graham of Northwestern and Eddie Prokop of Georgia Tech. He was widely credited with being the best faker of his day.

ABOVE: *In 1941, this Irish squad gathered for a chalk talk with head coach Frank Leahy. Two years later Notre Dame would be national champs.*

OPPOSITE TOP: *Notre Dame halfback (and later quarterback) Angelo Bertelli shakes off a tackler in 1941.*

OPPOSITE BOTTOM: *Johnny Lujack (32), star of the great 1943 team.*

Lujack was to prove himself Bertelli's equal. His first game, against Army, saw Lujack, an 18-year-old sophomore, direct the Irish to a 26-0 victory. Grantland Rice picked the 1943 Irish as the best Notre Dame team ever – a real mouthful, since that included the Four Horsemen of 1924 and Rockne's 1930 team with Frank Carideo.

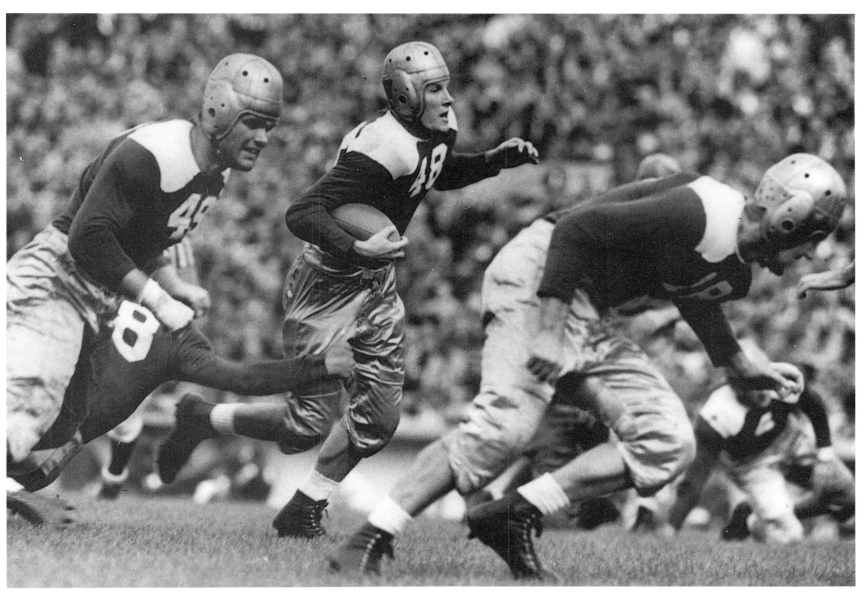

LEFT: *Coach Earl "Red" Blaik coached mighty Army to an undefeated season in 1944.*

OPPOSITE TOP: *Ready for Army: Notre Dame's Fighting Irish of 1945 prepare to meet the Cadets in Yankee Stadium.*

OPPOSITE BOTTOM: *Army's backfield wizards Doc Blanchard and Glenn Davis ("Mr. Outside" and "Mr. Inside").*

The success of the 1943 squad was all but forgotten everywhere but in South Bend the following year, as Leahy left for the service and Earl "Red" Blaik's 1944 Army team, with Glenn Davis and Doc Blanchard ("Mr Inside" and "Mr Outside") reigned supreme – that year and the next season as well. Army's 1944 Cadets demolished the Irish 59-0, and also trounced a mighty Navy team which many said was the best in the history of the Naval Academy. Blanchard and Davis won consecutive Heisman Trophies, in 1945 and 1946.

Coach Red Blaik received the following telegram just after the 1944 Army-Navy game, which Army won to cap its undefeated season:

The greatest of all Army teams. We have stopped the war to celebrate your magnificent success.
– Douglas MacArthur

But Coach Frank Leahy returned to Notre Dame in 1946, and until the end of the decade the Irish and Army continued their ferocious rivalry, which thoroughly dominated college football. In the Midwest Fritz Crisler's Michigan was a powerhouse, and Oklahoma, under coach Bud Wilkinson, was coming on strong – but either Notre Dame or Army was at the top every year but 1948, when the Michigan Wolverines were Number 1.

All-American Johnny Lujack was Notre Dame's star quarterback in 1946 and 1947, when he led the Irish to two consecutive national championships. He finally won the Heisman for Notre Dame in 1947. Other standouts on Leahy's teams of the late 1940s were linemen Johnny Mastrangelo, George Connor and George Strohmeyer, and guard Bill Fischer, in 1946; and halfbacks Terry Brennan and Emil "Six-Yard" Sitko, and tackle Ziggy Czarobski, in 1947.

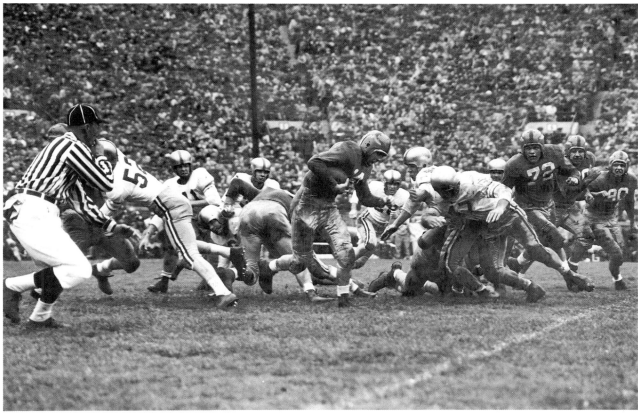

Despite the graduation of many of these stars, the 1948 and 1949 teams bounced back with giant end (and three-time All-America) Leon Hart, who was awarded the Heisman Trophy and the Maxwell Award in 1949. The 1948 Irish team had set an all-time attendance record of 580,268 fans for 10 games. Both teams were champions, and established Frank Leahy as a certified coaching genius – something Irish fans had known for years.

Leahy never attained the fame or celebrity of Knute Rockne – he lacked the Rock's winning personality – but he had racked up a truly amazing record since returning from the service. His 36 victories, two ties and no defeats accorded him the status of the most successful coach in the country – and recall that Notre Dame played the absolute best that the regional conferences had to offer.

It had beaten Southern Methodist, with its brilliant quarterback and living legend Doak Walker, and halfback Kyle Rote. It had beaten an inspired Southern California Trojan team. And it had annually jousted with Army.

However, Leahy was nothing if not a perfectionist. Joe Williams wrote of him in the *New York World-Telegram* in 1949:

What makes Leahy the most successful coach in the history of modern football? Material, of course, is the basic reason. Year in and year out Notre Dame probably gets the best material in the college world. But material is only part of the answer. Leahy has an extraordinary instinct and enthusiasm for football. He is satisfied with nothing short of perfection, and in striving to attain this he will drive himself, his assistants, and his players almost to a point of mental and physical exhaustion. To listen to him, none of his teams had ever turned in a perfect game.

The 1953 season saw the Irish undefeated again and ranked Number 1. Johnny Lattner was Notre Dame's star that year, a hardworking "bread and butter" halfback who ran and punted well, and whom Leahy called "a wonderful competitor" and "a fine clutch player." Lattner won both the Maxwell Award and the Heisman Trophy in 1953.

Little did Lattner, or any of the other Irish players, know that this would be Leahy's last season. The pressures of Notre Dame football and his own relentless perfectionism had taken their toll, and at halftime of the Georgia Tech game he collapsed with a "pancreatic attack." Upon the advice of his doctors, Frank Leahy retired as Notre Dame head coach on 31 January 1954. He had played for Knute Rockne, worked for him and learned football from him – but his coaching achievements stood on their own at Notre Dame.

The Golden Decade: The 1950s

The 1950s saw college football literally burst into full flower across the country. The United States was enjoying a postwar economic boom and football, both in the professional and college ranks, reflected the high spirits of the nation.

In 1953 a rule change forced the return of the one-platoon system in a modified form, with the elimination of free substitution, and suddenly teams which had dominated with offensive and defensive specialists had to regroup. Sixty-minute players were again the rule, and such teams as Ohio State, Maryland, Georgia Tech, Michigan State, Princeton, UCLA and West Virginia began to grab a little thunder from the likes of Notre Dame, Army and Michigan.

At Oklahoma, Bud Wilkinson's Sooners were cleaning up the Big Seven conference, fielding national championship teams in abundance, with superior depth and enough outstanding individual players to keep the fans excited.

The Big Ten was enjoying a happy decade, with Big Ten newcomer Michigan State achieving prominence under coach Clarence "Biggie" Munn and his successor, Duffy Daugherty. Iowa Hawkeye football was experiencing a resurgence under a dynamic new coach, former Wolverine star Forrest Evashevski. Ohio State, with players like Hopalong Cassady and Vic Janowicz, and a coach named Woody Hayes, was making the football world sit up and take notice.

ABOVE: *Iowa Hawkeye Alex Karras was an outstanding tackle in the 1950s, before he learned to act.*

RIGHT: *Wisconsin's Alan "The Horse" Ameche: a great running back.*

ABOVE: *Syracuse's Jim Brown, consensus All-American in 1956, still holds the record for the most points scored in a game (43).*

FAR LEFT: *Ohio State halfback Howard "Hopalong" Cassady, the 1955 Heisman Trophy winner.*

LEFT: *Triple-threat tailback Dick Kazmaier led the Princeton Tigers to two consecutive perfect seasons in 1950-51.*

For the Big Ten, it was a time of parity, a decade in which seven conference teams were to win or share the title. In fact, not until the late 1960s did the perennial battle begin between Ohio State and Michigan for mastery of the Big Ten.

The split T formation, developed by Don Faurot at Missouri, became fashionable in the 1950s. It was a decade of great backs as well. Besides Hopalong Cassady, there were exciting players such as Alan "The Horse" Ameche of Wisconsin, Johnny Lattner of Notre Dame, Jim Brown of Syracuse, and Billy Cannon of Louisiana State.

At Princeton, fans who had bemoaned the decline of Tiger football since the early glory days were cheering once again with the Princeton teams of 1950 and 1951 – coached by Charles Caldwell and led by triple-threat sensation Dick Kazmaier. He kicked, passed and ran for more than 4000 yards in three varsity seasons. He won the Heisman Trophy and the Maxwell Award, as well as All-America honors, in 1951.

A coach named Jim Tatum had arrived from Oklahoma to head the football program of the Maryland Terrapins, and by 1951 he had whipped them into a national power. Quarterback Jack Scarbath and the split T formation were Terrapin strengths that year, along with tackle Dick "Little Mo" Modzelewski. Maryland's 1953 team was perched atop the college football world, and Tatum was the toast of football, voted the Coach of the Year in the Scripps-Howard poll. Tatum eventually returned to coach his alma mater, North Carolina, but not before Maryland fans had gotten a taste of the good life.

The Rambling Wrecks of Georgia Tech, under Coach Bobby Dodd, electrified fans with the exploits of All-America linebacker and co-captain George Morris. The team was undefeated in 1952.

Thrills, upsets and new teams in the spotlight continued into the mid-1950s as two-way play again became the standard. The 1955 season in particular was a terrific one, highlighted by Oklahoma's continued domination with its colorful "fast-break" attack. But Michigan State, under Coach-of-the-Year Duffy Daugherty, was still thrashing Big Ten opponents, and edged out UCLA 17-14 in the Rose Bowl.

OPPOSITE: *The Maryland Terrapins were dominant in 1951, and quarterback Jack Scarbath was a big reason why.*

TOP: *Georgia Tech's 1952 team was undefeated under coach Bobby Dodd. They scored 301 points to their opponents' 52.*

LEFT: *The 1951 Maryland Terrapins in action.*

ABOVE: *Maryland coach Jim Tatum, voted Coach of the Year in 1953.*

TOP: *Perennial coach Lou Little of Columbia retired in 1956.*

BOTTOM: *The 1950s were good years for Michigan State fans under Duffy Daugherty, shown here with players Clinton Jones, Bob Apisa, Bubba Smith, Gene Washington and George Webster.*

RIGHT: *Notre Dame's "Golden Boy" Paul Hornung, shown here splitting the SMU line for the first touchdown of the 1955 Irish season.*

Maryland, UCLA, Ohio State, Texas Christian, Georgia Tech, Notre Dame, Auburn and Mississippi also fielded prominent teams that year. Pittsburgh took the Lambert Trophy as the top football team in the East in 1955.

The Southwest Conference continued to be unpredictable as favored SMU, Baylor and Rice wound up finishing far down in the conference, and Texas Christian and Texas A & M took first and second in 1955.

Meanwhile, the 1956 season had been set as the Ivy League's inaugural year as a formal conference. The eight members (Harvard, Princeton, Yale, Dartmouth, Cornell, Columbia, Pennsylvania and Brown) were to play a full round-robin for the very first time.

The 1956 season saw a subtle shift in college football as some perennial coaches announced retirement and a crop of big, fast and smart star players took the spotlight. Retiring were Lou Little of Columbia, after 27 years, Don Faurot of Missouri and Lynn "Pappy" Waldorf of California. Standout players that year included Notre Dame's Golden Boy, Heisman Trophy winner Paul Hornung. Jim Brown of Syracuse, Johnny Majors of Tennessee, Michigan's Ron Kramer and Oklahoma's Tommy McDonald also exemplified the new breed of college player. Speed and smarts were their hallmark.

These players, and others who graduated in the late 1950s, were perhaps the first who had dedicated themselves to football as a lifetime pursuit. Top college players in the late 1950s knew they would turn professional, and their dedication to physical conditioning, studying the game and learning from top coaches reflected that change in attitude. Football had long ceased to be a pleasant way to while away Saturday afternoons for these athletes.

The end of the golden decade of the 1950s featured the NCAA rules committee instituting the two-point conversion and liberalizing the substitution rule to an extent where two-platoon football was again possible. Blocking rules were tightened so as to permit only the hand or arm to be used.

The end of the decade also saw the renewal of the Army-Notre Dame rivalry for the first time since 1947, Army's "lonely end" attack with Bill Carpenter, Red Blaik's retirement from Army after the 1958 season, and the shocking disbanding of the Pacific Coast Conference. The Big Ten-PCC Rose Bowl agreement was also ended, although Big Ten teams could still play at Pasadena if they so chose. There was also some discussion of forming a coast-to-coast conference of major independents.

Outstanding players lighting up college football as the decade drew to a close included Louisiana State's Billy Cannon, Charlie Flowers of Mississippi, Army's Pete Dawkins and Randy Duncan of Iowa. Two new Bowls, the Liberty and the Bluebonnet, made their debut in 1959.

Football in the 1950s had sauntered by with the rest of the decade. Now it was time for the game, like the United States itself, to enter the Space Age.

ABOVE: *TCU's Marshall Robinson takes out a blocker and a runner in the 1952 game against Texas A & M. The Southwest Conference was unpredictable in the 1950s.*

RIGHT: *Army's Pete Dawkins was a sensation in 1958, the year he won the Heisman Trophy and Maxwell Award. He went on to attend Oxford on a Rhodes Scholarship.*

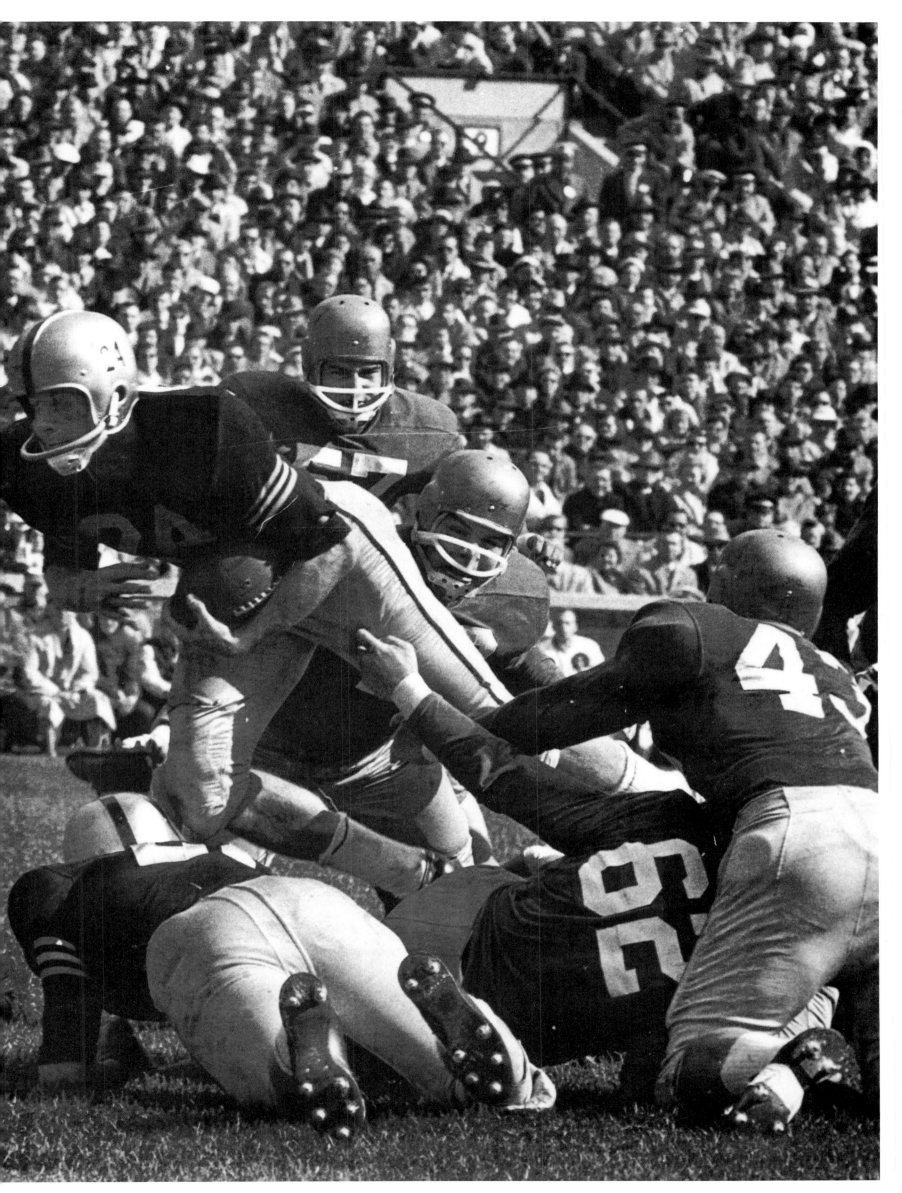

A 1960s college football album:

RIGHT: *John McKay, USC's master football coach of the 1960s and early 1970s. He turned out four national championship teams.*

BOTTOM LEFT: *Ted Kennedy as a Harvard footballer in the 1960s.*

BOTTOM RIGHT: *Mike Adamle, Northwestern's star of the late 1960s, went on to broadcasting.*

OPPOSITE TOP: *Kenny Stabler, who played for Alabama under Bear Bryant, goes for extra yardage against Nebraska in 1966.*

OPPOSITE BOTTOM: *Missouri's 1960 team won the Big Eight Conference Championship before the decade belonged to Nebraska.*

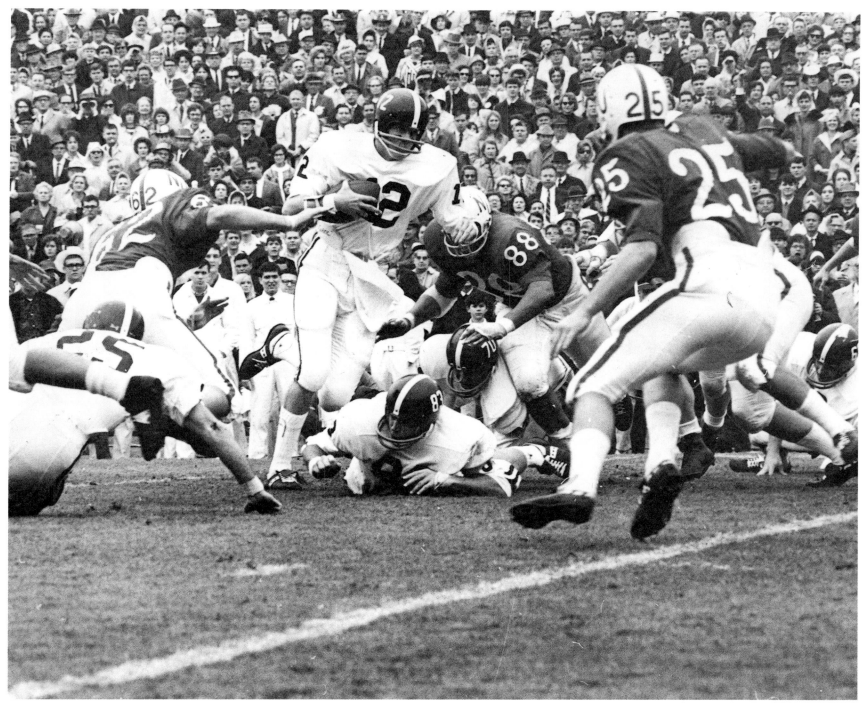

TOP: *Gale Sayers in a slashing run for Kansas in the early 1960s.*

ABOVE: *Defensive back Johnny Roland consults with coach Dan Devine at Missouri, circa 1965.*

RIGHT: *Bob Griese, the king of football at Purdue from 1964 to 1966, was the Heisman runner-up in 1966.*

OPPOSITE: *Wildman Bobby Douglass, Kansas' quarterback in the late 1960s.*

Oklahoma and the Big Seven

ABOVE: *Bud Wilkinson of Oklahoma Sooners coaching fame. He was so popular he could have run for office – and did.*

OPPOSITE TOP: *Oklahoma's halfback Clendon Thomas was the nation's leading scorer in 1956, with runs like this one.*

BELOW: *The undefeated 1949 Oklahoma Sooners team, part of Wilkinson's incredible winning streak of 31 consecutive games.*

Bud Wilkinson's Oklahoma Sooners dominated their conference, and indeed college football as a whole, from the late 1940s to the mid-1950s. In a sense, they also epitomized the spirit of heartland football. Then the Big Seven (Kansas, Missouri, Nebraska, Kansas State, Iowa State, Oklahoma State and Colorado), now the Big Eight (Oklahoma State jumped on the bandwagon in 1958), this big, brawny Midwestern conference is, in the eyes of many fans, the quintessential college football conference. The rivalries are ferocious, the fans raucous, and the brand of football compares with the best anywhere.

In the introduction to his book *Big Eight Football*, football historian John D McCallum comments on the spirit of the Big Eight:

Ever since Nebraska started playing Notre Dame in 1915 (Cornhuskers 20, Fighting Irish 19), everyone who follows the Big Eight has had somebody he especially likes to see beaten. During the week of their game, Nebraska feels about Oklahoma the way Yale feels about Harvard. Beneath the breast of every Kansas bass drummer lies a hatred for Missouri. Whirl a Colorado man around several times and he'll stagger straight to Lincoln, Nebraska, with a couple of buckets of silver and gold paint, if the cardinal and gold of Iowa State hasn't already beaten him there. Give an Oklahoma State supporter a few drinks, and he'll bet all the beef on the hoof he's got that the OSU Cowboys will whip the Sooners.

It is difficult to describe how completely Coach Bud Wilkinson and the Oklahoma Sooners ruled football, except by simply relating the amazing statistics: Between 1948 and 1957, the Big Seven Conference had only one champion – Oklahoma. After losing the first game of the 1948 season to Santa Clara, Oklahoma won 31 games in a row before finally losing to Kentucky in the 1951 Sugar Bowl.

An even more stunning streak began in 1953 in the third game of the season against Texas, which the Sooners won 19-14. Wilkinson and Oklahoma steamrolled their gridiron competition for the next 47 games in a row, their next loss coming with a 7-0 upset by Notre Dame in November of 1957 – a collegiate record which many football experts feel will never be broken.

Such was the fame of Charles "Bud" Wilkinson in his 17 years as head coach of Oklahoma that he really could have "run for public office" – and indeed he did, leaving Oklahoma at age 50 after the 1963 season to make an unsuccessful bid for the US Senate. He eventually headed up John F Kennedy's President's Physical Fitness Program, and later served in an executive post for President Richard Nixon. If he had stayed at Oklahoma, he would have stood an excellent chance of ranking among the winningest coaches of all time – his 17-year record stands at 145 wins, 29 losses and 4 ties.

Tall, handsome and a former star quarterback and guard on Bernie Bierman's 1934-36 Minnesota teams, Wilkinson himself had a rare combination of personal charm and motivational genius. His players idolized him and gave him their very best effort.

Bud Wilkinson was not, strictly speaking, a football innovator but he believed in the virtues of bone-jarring power. And he possessed not only a sharp mind but an all-business attitude which was devoid of affectations, and perfectly fit the times in which he coached. The "wizard of Norman" usually dressed in a white shirt and loosely-knotted tie, looking more like a displaced executive prowling the sideline than a football coach.

Wilkinson had his share of All-America players in those years of glory, but only once did he coach a Heisman winner – halfback Billy Vessels in 1952. Instead, his teams seemed to be composed mainly of steady, above-average players at each position, who played astonishingly well as a team – the mark of a great coach.

Individual and team honors during those miraculous years stack up like this: Oklahoma was awarded the national championship three times, in 1950, 1955 and 1956. Four Sooner teams were unbeaten: those of 1949, 1950, 1954 and 1955. Wilkinson was named Coach-of-the-Year in 1949. His Bowl record was 6-2, including four victories in the Orange Bowl.

Oklahoma has won national championships since, under Barry Switzer (in 1974 and 1975), and has continued to dominate the Big Eight along with archrival Nebraska. However, Bud Wilkinson's shadow is still a long one on the great plains near the town of Norman, Oklahoma.

RIGHT: *Darrell Royal sweeps Nebraska's end in 1947 as Oklahoma won, 14-13. He would go on to coaching success himself.*

BELOW LEFT: *Halfback Billy Vessels was Wilkinson's only Heisman winner, in 1952.*

BELOW RIGHT: *Coach Wilkinson with Oklahoma's 1957 co-captains, Clendon Thomas (left) and Don Stiller.*

OPPOSITE TOP: *Oklahoma continues to dominate the Big Eight, along with archrival Nebraska.*

OPPOSITE BOTTOM LEFT: *Barry Switzer became Oklahoma's head coach in 1973, and resigned under pressure in 1989.*

OPPOSITE BOTTOM RIGHT: *Oklahoma halfback Steve Owens was awarded the 1969 Heisman Trophy for great ball-carrying like this.*

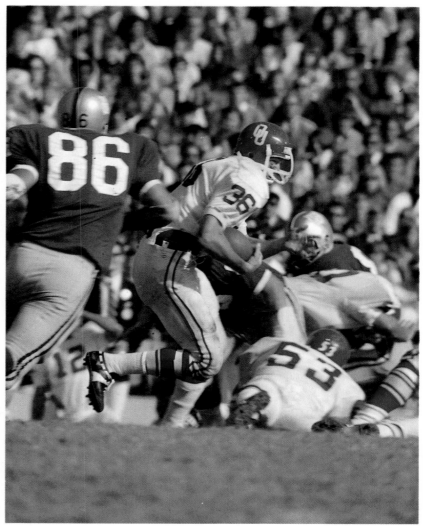

Fans, Bands, and Fun in the Stands

As the game of football has evolved, so has the art of watching the game. From the first college game, when the spectators took a spill off the wooden fence during a player collision, football stadiums have become giant concrete affairs which hold 100,000 fans or more. As the crowds have grown, a complex social framework has sprung up to cheer the football team on and add to the enjoyment of those in the stands.

From early days of watching the game from one's carriage – in a bowler hat, and clapping politely – fans have progressed through raccoon coats and tiny pennants to today's roaring multitudes, faces painted in the school colors and banners waving defiantly. It's not enough any more just to beat one's opponent on the gridiron. Competition over whose cheerleaders are prettier, whose marching band is more lively, and whose fight song can be sung louder, add spice and interest for those who aren't actually playing the game.

Fight songs, usually composed by alumni with an ear for music and sentimental lyrics, have been sung (or yelled) since the turn of the century. Many of these pieces have become as familiar as old classics. Most football fans can hum the Michigan fight song even if they didn't go to Ann Arbor and don't know the words. And most Indiana children grow up hearing the Notre Dame Victory March as often as "Happy Birthday." In the Midwest, a thriving market exists for automobile horns which play the first stanza of a particular fight song when the horn is sounded. Many collegians graduate without ever having learned the words to their school's Alma Mater, but having sung the fight song a thousand times.

TOP: *Ohio State's drum major struts his stuff.*

RIGHT: *Maryland's drummers look cool even on the hottest fall day.*

OPPOSITE: *Penn State's Nittany Lion marching band incites excitement in the stands: it's all part of a sunny Saturday afternoon.*

ABOVE: *A 1931 USC collegiate wins the honor of appearing as a Trojan in full armor in ceremonies officially opening the football season.*

RIGHT: *Jack Snow and John Huarte of the 1964 Fighting Irish pose in front of the bronze statue of "We're Number One" Moses.*

Not long after the fight songs, no doubt, came the marching bands. Modelling their original uniforms and choreography after those of military bands, marching bands and halftime shows have become as much a part of Saturday afternoon as the kickoff. Arrayed in the school colors, marching bands are usually composed of music students, lovers of drama, and other assorted free spirits, and they seem to have different styles according to regional tradition. Big Ten and Big Eight marching bands go for large numbers, complicated choreography and flashy drum majors, with twirlers and flag lines added for good measure. Traditional military-style uniforms are the rule.

In the South and Southwest, however, a definite jazz flavor permeates the style of playing of many bands, with bowler hats and large horn sections the rule.

Alumni bands are becoming more popular – not just as a feature of the Homecoming Weekend halftime show but all year round. They are an easy and fun way to increase band participation, and court local alumni who remember the marching band fondly and still have the old horn or drum somewhere up in the attic.

No one knows which football team had the first official cheerleaders, but they go way back. Today's cheerleading squads are likely to pair college men with women, and thrilling acrobatics are usually featured along with leading the crowds in cheers and in the fight song.

Team nicknames do have a definite origin. In 1877 Princeton named its footballers the "Tigers" because of the orange-and-black stockings they wore in the games. Some team names harken back to ancient lore of the area, such as Iowa's Hawkeyes (named for the scout in James Fenimore Cooper's *Last of the Mohicans*) or Penn State's Nittany Lions (mythical animals who live in the Nittany Mountains.)

Some are names denoting fierceness, such as the Lions, Wildcats, Badgers, Wolverines, Tigers, Bears and Bulldogs. Georgia claims it was the first to call their Bulldogs "Dawgs," and to print up the thousands of bumper stickers and signs asking, "How 'Bout Them Dawgs?"

Not all team nicknames are that easy to visualize. The North Carolina Tarheels, the Indiana Hoosiers, the Purdue Boilermakers (a reference to the school's large student population of mechanical engineers),

ABOVE: *A classic Harvard University archives photo of 1887 students watching the game. Style was always part of being a spectator.*

BELOW: *Alumni marching bands, such as Northwestern's "Numbalums," have become a fun way to extend school spirit – and musicianship – beyond the collegiate years.*

RIGHT: *In 1927 there were no female cheerleaders at Marquette University in Milwaukee, but that didn't stop this rooter for the Golden Avalanche.*

TOP: *USC's blonde cheerleaders are informally and perennially judged the nation's most beautiful.*

OPPOSITE: *Ohio State's card section keeps the fans involved – and occupied.*

ABOVE: *Pom-pon girls are part of the pomp and pageantry, such as at the 1984 Rose Bowl game featuring the University of Illinois.*

and the Hawaii Rainbow Warriors are among them. Other team names refer to historical events – like the Oklahoma Sooners who settled the state and the Tennessee Volunteers who "volunteered" to fight in the Civil War.

Mascots, real or impersonated, are another way to add fun and cheer on the team. Many are the overheated underclassmen who have paraded around in Wildcat, Hawkeye, Buckeye, Cowboy, Indian and Tiger outfits. But pity even more the cheerleaders who get to lead the Colorado Buffalo around: It's a real one! So is the Texas Longhorn steer. Real bulldogs, of course, are revered mascots at several schools, as are real Saluki dogs (Egyptian greyhounds) at Southern Illinois University. A succession of real goats, always named Billy, have been the treasured mascot of the Navy Midshipmen.

Illiniwek the Indian Chief, at the University of Illinois, and the USC Trojan are students who have the honor of portraying the school symbol – the Trojan even rides a real white horse.

OPPOSITE: *Penn State fans take their school colors seriously.*

TOP: *Bulldogs are a popular mascot at many schools. Here, Yale's student mascot and a bulldog take a breather together on the sideline at a 1981 game.*

LEFT: *The Clemson Tiger is a part of the tradition at that well-known football school – as is the tiger-paw print on flags, faces and pennants.*

ABOVE: *The mascot of the Miami Hurricanes, fiercely overlooking the festivities.*

Bonfires are coming back into fashion after having been frowned upon by school administrators for some years. Burning effigies of the opposing players add to the general mayhem of a pep rally.

Pep rallies are exemplified by the student conclave at Notre Dame's Stepan Center the Friday night before every game. Often televised since the Irish have attained prominence again under Coach Lew Holtz, the pep rally features cheerleaders, victory predictions by the football team and Coach Holtz, and the singing of the Victory March.

Tailgating is one of the most honored traditions among alumni. Four simple repasts in picnic baskets brought to the field where the game would be held, tailgate parties have evolved into full-fledged outdoor banquets complete with candelabra, fully-stocked bars, huge motor homes painted in the school colors, and alumni fans decked out in all their gaudy finery. At a tailgate before a Harvard-Yale game, you might spot a chauffeured Rolls Royce or two. Before the Texas-Oklahoma game, you might be treated to chicken-fried steaks, chili and Pearl beer.

The Nittany Lion has been splashed with orange paint by Syracuse Orangemen fans, USC's Tommy Trojan statue has been found without his sword before a UCLA game, and the Notre Dame faithful must have their picture taken in front of the statue of Moses, with his finger pointed upward in a gesture they interpret as meaning that "God Made Notre Dame Number 1!"

It's all in the name of school spirit.

OPPOSITE TOP: *The "Big Drum" of the Texas Longhorn marching band is at home in larger-than-life Texas.*

OPPOSITE BOTTOM: *Dotting the "i" at Ohio State – the greatest honor which can be bestowed on a Buckeye marching band member.*

RIGHT: *Twin twirlers at Purdue University, home of the "Golden Girl," where twirling is a way of life.*

BELOW: *Notre Dame's marching band features Irish dancers in full regalia.*

OPPOSITE: *Notre Dame football players charging out of the tunnel to the "Victory March" – the greatest entrance in college football.*

ABOVE: *Purdue's marching band, one of the biggest in the country, features comely kickers.*

LEFT: *Tradition reigns at Dartmouth, where cheerleading attire, formations and megaphones recall the 1950s. This photo was taken in 1983.*

Bryant, Paterno, and Hayes: Three Ways To Win

Only rarely does a college football coach establish a legend so enormous that it overshadows the football team itself. Although Woody Hayes of Ohio State, Joe Paterno of Penn State, and Bear Bryant of Alabama have all been extremely successful coaches, their legends lie in a unique approach to life, the influence they have had on the game and on their players, and their unshakable personal self-confidence.

These three coaching legends have displayed radically different styles: Hayes was a sideline tantrum-thrower who nonetheless earned the undying devotion of his players; Paterno, still at the helm at Penn State, is a thoughtful man who is keenly aware of football's place in society as a whole; and Bear Bryant was the type of larger-than-life figure who inspired George Blanda to think to himself when he first met him, "This must be what God looks like." Between them, they've won 10 Coach-of-the-Year awards.

Bear Bryant

"I'm just a plow hand from Arkansas," he once told *Time* magazine. "But I've learned over the years how to hold a team together. How to lift some men up, how to calm down others, until finally they've got one heartbeat together, a team."

Born poor in the cotton fields of Arkansas, Paul W "Bear" Bryant arrived at Alabama to coach football in 1958, after successful stints at Maryland (1945), Kentucky (1946-53) and Texas A & M (1954-57). His lifetime coaching record stands at 323 wins, 85 losses and 17 ties. (Bryant hated tie games most of all, and is credited with the axiom, "A

tie is like kissing your sister" – but he claims he heard it first from Jim Tatum at Maryland.) Only Eddie Robinson, still coaching at Grambling, has surpassed Bryant's record for all-time victories.

Bryant coached his share of free spirits, like Babe Parilli, Joe Namath (Bryant called him "Joe Willie") and Kenny Stabler. He seemed to know how to motivate these future stars without breaking their spirits.

Bryant had a deep personal sense of loyalty. Although he had been happy and revered at Texas A & M in the mid-1950s, his name kept coming up when there was a vacancy at Alabama – the Bear's alma mater. Finally, after a tough loss to archrival Texas, Bryant called the reporters in and explained his position:

There is one and only one reason that I would consider (the Alabama job). . . . When you were playing as a kid, say you heard your mother call you. If you thought she just wanted you to do some chores, or come in for supper, you might not answer her. But if you thought she needed you, you'd be there in a hurry.

It became known as the "Mama Called" speech – and with that, Bryant was off to Alabama.

He became the most revered personage in the state. He had a rare ability to remain homey and still hobnob with presidents, senators and rich boosters. He endorsed politicians for public office in the state of Alabama. TV sportscasters loved him for his quotability. He formed

LEFT: *The Bear prowls the sideline in his famous hat, surrounded by his beloved Crimson Tide players. He was one of the most famous and revered college coaches who ever lived.*

OPPOSITE: *Coach Bryant is hoisted up by jubilant players after breaking Pop Warner's record.*

LEFT: *Notre Dame coach Ara Parseghian tries on Bryant's hat for size as the two teams meet for the 1975 Orange Bowl. Notre Dame won, 13-11.*

BELOW LEFT: *"This must be what God looks like," thought George Blanda when he first met Bryant.*

OPPOSITE TOP: *Future Penn State coach Joe Paterno as he appeared on Brown University's team, circa 1949.*

OPPOSITE BOTTOM: *A coach's triumph: Paterno is carried off the field after Penn State defeated Pitt in 1974, 31-10, to capture the Number 1 standing.*

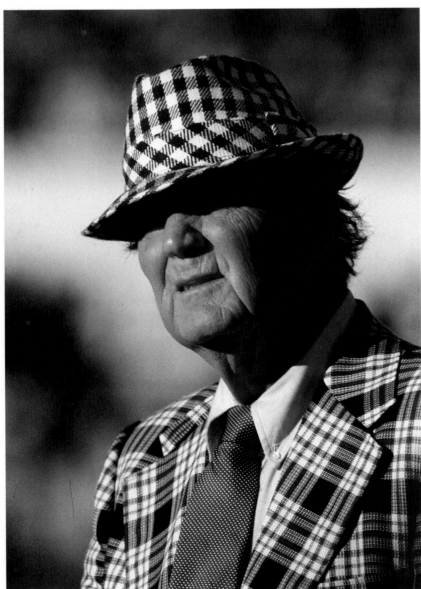

solid friendships with many of his rival coaches and other prominent ones not on the Crimson Tide's schedule: Bud Wilkinson, Woody Hayes, and Eddie Robinson among them.

The Bear was certainly not without his faults. He had a drinking problem, and finally licked it. He smoked and ate too much, gambled, and was implicated in a recruitment scandal. He didn't coach a black player until 1974 – not because he was prejudiced against blacks himself, say his fans, but because for many years he followed the policies of the schools where he coached.

At a star-studded testimonial dinner given late in Bryant's career, old players streamed back to tell stories and relive the old days. They still called him "Coach Bryant" – even the ones in their fifties and sixties.

Bryant often said when he quit coaching he would die. He died suddenly, in 1983 at the age of 69, less than a month after his final victory, over Illinois in the Liberty Bowl.

Joe Paterno

"There are other things in life besides football." Those are unusual words coming from a college football coach, but Joe Paterno of Penn State is not your usual football coach.

Paterno has become the undisputed thinking man's football coach, a genuine intellectual who was dissuaded from pursuing a law career by Penn State coach Charles A "Rip" Engle, in favor of a career in coaching. He arrived at University Park, Pennsylvania in 1966 and, as of the 1988 season, has not endured a losing season. His current record stands at 212 wins, 52 losses and 2 ties. Enormously popular with Penn State collegians, Paterno often strolls the campus, easily accessible to students and happy to engage in conversation about football, philosophy or any other subject.

As he creeps up the list of all-time winningest active coaches with his Nittany Lions, Paterno has expressed his views on recruiting, on scholar-athletes, and on many other issues confronting college football. Here are some of them, as quoted in the book *Joe Paterno: Football My Way* by Merv Hyman and Gordon White.

On discipline:

I believe in discipline but I think that a coach's rules have to be tempered to consider the player. What difference does it make how long a kid's hair is? That doesn't have one single thing to do with discipline. When it comes to hair, dress or living habits, I think college football players are old enough and men enough to handle these things themselves. There are some things, however, that must remain the prerogative of the coach, like how long we're going to practice, who's going to play and what we're going to do in a game. That is one area where I think a coach cannot be adjustable if football is to survive as a part of college life.

On the game itself:

Football is a great game. It demands a young man's total commitment – emotionally, mentally and physically. It challenges our young people to do their very best, to discipline themselves to develop mental, as well as physical, toughness. At its best it is a wonderful and worthwhile experience, which will have immense future character benefits for its players. But it must be at its best to continue to be meaningful for our young people of today. Its intrinsic essence of hard work and honest competition should not be polluted by hypocritical actions of its leaders and coaches. Its character benefits should not be diluted by dishonest and misleading recruiting procedures. We should not at any time let any of its participants be exploited for the personal ambition of any man or institution. . . . I have spoken frankly, with high hopes that perhaps this effort will help call attention to some of the malpractices which should be eliminated from the game I love – intercollegiate football.

ABOVE: *Paterno after his 200th win at Penn State.*

ABOVE RIGHT: *Sugar Bowl fans in 1983 cast their vote for Coach-of-the-Year. Paterno in fact won that honor for the 1982-83 season.*

RIGHT: *Woody Hayes, surrounded by a sea of Buckeye red and gray, holds forth on the way to win.*

OPPOSITE: *A force of nature stalking the sideline: Wayne Woodrow Hayes.*

Woody Hayes

"Without winners, there wouldn't be any civilization." That, in a nutshell, was the life philosophy of Wayne Woodrow Hayes, known as "Woody" throughout Ohio and the nation. From 1951 to 1978, Hayes coached the Ohio State Buckeyes to three national championships (1954, 1957 and 1968) and 14 Big Ten titles either won or shared with archrival Michigan. Before Ohio State, Hayes had served apprenticeships at Denison (1946-48) and Miami of Ohio (1949-1950). His career record is 238 wins, 72 losses and 10 ties.

Hayes, as much as any other Big Ten coach, was responsible for the "three yards and a cloud of dust" offensive style that characterized Big Ten football for decades and reached its zenith at Ohio State. Wary of passing, and favoring players who excelled at grind-it-out football, Hayes was criticized for a somewhat monotonous playbook, as well as for excluding non-conference powerhouses such as Notre Dame, Oklahoma and Nebraska from Ohio State's schedule each year. Yet Ohio State fans adored him and retorted that there was nothing monotonous about winning football games.

TOP: *Hayes barks out orders as he lines his Ohio State players up for the team photo in 1975.*

RIGHT: *Woody could be a gentle and generous person too.*

OPPOSITE: *Coach Hayes leaves no doubt in Buckeye Rex Kern's mind as to what the next play should be. Kern was a Heisman runner-up in 1969.*

His style of coaching and his motivational tactics were legendary. Hayes had a ferocious temper and players who made mistakes were not the only targets. Sportswriters, officials, and opposing players and coaches were sometimes caught up in his wildly emotional reactions.

During a game against Michigan in 1971 (the biggest game of every Buckeye season), Hayes grabbed the yard markers from some officials he considered derelict in their duties, and broke them over his knee, tossing them onto the field in contempt. Stories of Woody punching photographers, yelling at journalists during interviews and swinging at opposing players mounted as his years at OSU passed.

Yet Woody could be a kind and gentle man. Stories of him sending money to former players so they could finish their education, or bailing out old friends in trouble, and singlehandedly supporting a multitude of charitable causes, are as numerous as the "Woody took a swing at me" stories.

Hayes had no illusions about the job security of the college football coaching profession. "I had a Cadillac offered to me a couple of times," he recalled. "You know how that works. They give you a Cadillac one year and the next year they give you the gas to get out of town." Several times he turned down pay increases, insisting that the money be given to his assistants.

In 1978, Woody made the mistake that cost him his job. During the Gator Bowl, against Clemson, with the Buckeyes trailing 17-15, Clemson linebacker Charlie Bauman intercepted an Ohio State pass and tumbled out of bounds almost at Hayes' feet. Enraged, Hayes began screaming at Bauman and struck him on the face mask. When a member of his own team tried to restrain him, Hayes turned and punched him. The next day, he was fired from his position as head football coach at Ohio State University.

Woody Hayes is often held up as a coaching example – either good or bad. In his single-minded determination to win, and in his dedication to Ohio State football, there is much to admire. Too often, however, he allowed that determination to cloud his personal and professional judgement. It's safe to say, however, that the primary victim of his coaching excesses was himself. Still, his career record places him among the five winningest coaches ever.

Rivalries

Every college football team has its archrival, the team they hate, the one they would rather die young than lose to. Coaches point toward it, students prepare for it, alumni come back for it, and riots break out over it. Sometimes it's an interconference rivalry. Sometimes two teams in the same state battle over bragging rights. Sometimes their fans just don't like each other.

The Texas-Oklahoma game has been described as "a prison riot with coeds" by Dan Jenkins of *Sports Illustrated*. There is no home field advantage because the game is always held at the Cotton Bowl. There is no crowd advantage either – an equal number, it seems, of oil men, politicians and assorted millionaires shows up to root for each team. It's just one of those grudge matches which makes college football what it is, and it's been going on since the turn of the century, when the annual contest became part of the Texas State Fair.

In John D McCallum's book *Big Eight Football*, he describes the game between Oklahoma and its chief non-conference rival:

It is one of the maddest spectacles of sport. The game is played in the Cotton Bowl, with 76,000 seats of the stadium crammed with the loudest, most animated partisans in college football, evenly divided between Texans and Oklahomans. Regardless of the team records, the excitement is there each year. Just before the game's kickoff a few years ago, fullback Harold Phillipp of Texas, talking about the Texas boys playing for Oklahoma, compared the Texas defectors to American soldiers playing for Germany during World War II. During the contest an immense roar wafts up from the stadium on every play, and the two large bands play 'Boomer Sooner,' the Oklahoma fight song, and 'Texas Fight,' the Longhorns' song, over and over again, always to the accompaniment of a cheering, jeering mob of singers. More often than not, the action in the stands matches the fighting on the field.

Contrast that scene with the annual battle between Harvard and Yale, which is an older rivalry by far, and one taken a bit more seriously in terms of honor and glory.

A Yale coach once addressed his team in the mid-1920s before the Big Game: "Gentlemen, you are about to play football for Yale against Harvard. Never in your lives will you do anything so important."

ABOVE: *The University of Michigan marching band has a message for Ohio State coach Woody Hayes, during a classic matchup between the two Big Ten archrivals.*

LEFT: *A friendly moment between Hayes and Wolverine coach Bo Schembechler before the annual hostilities begin.*

OPPOSITE: *Lonely are the brave: Above the torrent of Buckeye partisans, Michigan fans unfurl their banner.*

ABOVE: *Where college football rivalries began: the Ivy League. Here, the 1985 Harvard-Yale game at the Yale Bowl.*

RIGHT: *The famous 29-29 "win" of Harvard over Yale, 1968. Here, Harvard's reserve QB Frank Champi tosses a pass. His TD toss with three seconds to go, followed by a PAT, grabbed a tie.*

RIGHT: *Yale's quarterback Brian Dowling was a big reason the Elis were undefeated that 1968 season.*

In 1937, Franklin P Adams, wit and philosopher and a charter member of the Algonquin Round Table, had this to say about the boredom of listening to Harvard and Yale fans discussing the game:

About Tuesday you read the ballyhoo. Harvard, spurred by last Saturday's staggering defeat, has a fighting chance against Yale. Thursday one of the Yale stars has galloping rigor mortis and may be out of the game ten days. Saturday morning he is on crutches or in a wheelchair, and that afternoon he plays the Game of His Life.

Not all of the glory attendant upon the Big Game belongs to the past. In 1968, both teams were, surprisingly, undefeated going into the annual contest. Harvard's strong defense would take on Yale's celebrated quarterback Brian Dowling and halfback Calvin Hill.

With all of 42 seconds left in the game, Yale led 29-13. Reporters had their story leads prepared on the defeat of the Harvard Crimson. Then, in a turn of events that could only have happened in the Harvard-Yale game, Harvard scored a touchdown, a two-point conversion and another touchdown just as time ran out. With the game clock reading "0," Harvard's Crimson managed another two-point conversion to tie the score and send the Yale fans home shaking their heads. The next day's *Crimson* carried the headline proclaiming the moral victory, "Harvard Beats Yale, 29-29."

The gridiron battles between the two service academies, Army and

Navy, have been noteworthy not only for intense football but also for great pranks, banners and mascots. Perhaps it is the only college football rivalry of which it can be said that the competition has professional overtones as well as athletic. Army and Navy men will spend a lifetime in more or less friendly competition – why not act it out on the gridiron?

The rivalry began in 1890 with the Naval Academy's challenge to West Point, which had no team, to a game of soccer-style football. Army's best athletes took a crash course in football and prepared to meet Navy. A mascot was picked up along the way when the Middies commandeered a goat en route. Not surprisingly, however, Navy trounced the Cadets 24-0. Miffed, the Cadets issued a challenge for a rematch the following year and avenged their loss, 32-16.

Since then, the rivalry has had its ups and downs. A verbal brawl between Army and Navy brass after the 1893 contest, which ended in a challenge to a duel, prompted President Grover Cleveland to ban future games between the two academies. The ban was observed until 1899, when the football rivalry was renewed by mutual agreement. Stops also occurred after an Army player died in 1909 during a game, in 1917 and 1918 during World War I, and in 1928 and 1929 when the two schools could not agree on eligibility requirements for players.

Modern Army-Navy games have assumed national importance – at least in the eyes of the combatants. The ritualized marching and drilling of each academy, in full uniform, before each game is quite a spectacle. Football historians claim the game's first scalpers did business

Harvard-Yale
November 20 1926

before Army-Navy contests. The games have usually been held in Philadelphia – most recently at Veterans Stadium, which can hold the huge numbers of fans who want to see the game. In 1926, another large football venue – Chicago's Soldier Field – was dedicated with an Army-Navy game.

Great pranks have been pulled at the annual Army-Navy classic. In 1946, President Harry Truman and a crowd of 100,000 fans saw a large group of what looked like Army cheerleaders pull an enormous wooden goat onto the field – out of a trap door in the "Trojan Goat" stepped Billy X (the latest in the unbroken line of Navy mascots). The cheerleaders then pulled off their Army outfits to reveal Navy uniforms.

However, Navy's surprise failed to alter the outcome of the game against the superb Army Cadets, led by Doc Blanchard and coached by Red Blaik. They rallied mightily late in the game, but still lost, after a last-minute play on Army's three-yard line failed when the crowd surged onto the field and time expired. Army won 21-18.

Chicago residents know, without being told, when Notre Dame is hosting their annual showdown with USC: Because the USC fans stop off in the Windy City, in full Trojan regalia, before the morning drive to South Bend. They crowd the restaurants, bend elbows on Rush Street, and tell anyone within shouting distance that they'll whip the Fighting Irish. For their part, Notre Dame always seems to make a special effort to have windy, raw weather on hand to welcome the Californians.

Since 1926, when Howard Jones issued a personal invitation to Knute Rockne to come west so USC could "beat the best," the two teams have fought, kicked and clawed – seemingly for no reason other than a decades-long grudge. Ara Parseghian's admirable career at the helm of Notre Dame was marred by six losses to USC, against three wins and two ties.

TOP: *The Harvard-Yale football game, 1926. The annual contest has offered a fashionable afternoon's entertainment for more than 100 years.*

ABOVE: *Ara Parseghian at Notre Dame in 1971. His fine record as coach of the Irish was marred by several losses to hated rival USC.*

RIGHT: *Notre Dame grabs a pass as a sea of Army Cadets looks on, during the 1966 edition of this classic rivalry.*

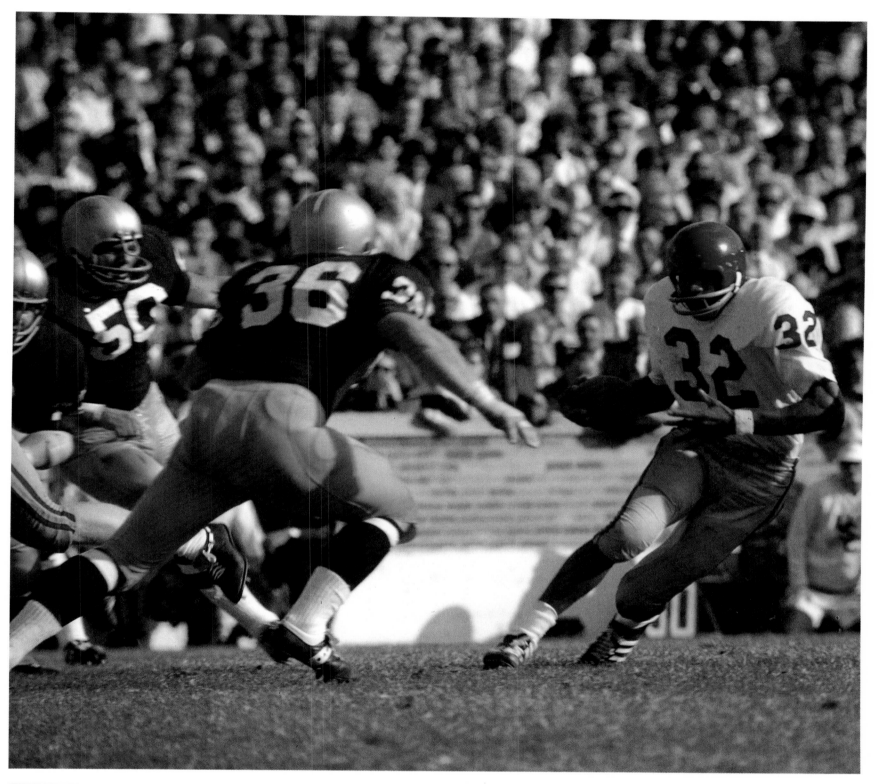

ABOVE: *Trojan O.J. Simpson puts the moves on Notre Dame defenders during a 1967 game between USC and the Irish.*

LEFT: *The Trojan marching band adds fuel to the fire with their stirring play and uniforms.*

139

The 1978 contest featured USC under coach John Robinson, rated Number 1, needing only to beat Notre Dame to win the title. The Trojans led 17-3 at the half, when in the third quarter, Irish quarterback Joe Montana erupted for four touchdowns with his brilliant passing plays, and Notre Dame led 25-24. Yet USC clawed back to field goal range in the final 41 seconds, and Frank Jordan booted a 37-yard shot which gave the Trojans a 27-25 victory. *New York Times* columnist Red Smith called it "the gaudiest game in the 50 years of the rivalry."

When Michigan and Ohio State get together, it's the biggest game of the year for both teams, unless one of them gets into the Rose Bowl. And since the Big Ten has not fared well in the Rose Bowl lately, even more importance is attached to the yearly Michigan-Ohio State game.

Woody Hayes would do everything but scrawl "Beat Michigan" across his forehead in blood to motivate his Buckeyes, while Michigan's Bo Schembechler probably blames at least half of his cardiac incidents on the tension of battling Ohio State.

The Wolverines won the first duel in 1897, 34-0. When Hayes took over at Ohio State in the early 1950s, Michigan had pretty much dominated the annual contest. Hayes began reversing that trend almost as a holy quest. Over the next 25 years, the Buckeyes went 16-8-1 against the hated Wolverines. Schembechler, who had played for Hayes at Miami of Ohio and served as an assistant coach under him at OSU for four years, swept Hayes' last three seasons up until the Clemson incident in 1978.

The 1979 game saw the Buckeyes led by their new coach Earle Bruce, and it turned out to be a typical heartstopping game. It would decide the Big Ten title and the Rose Bowl bid – as so many Michigan-Ohio State games had before. Michigan hosted, and 106,255 fans turned out to see the action.

Earle Bruce had swept aside Hayes' grind-it-out rushing style in favor of a passing attack led by his flashy quarterback Art Schlichter,

LEFT: *The 1926 Army-Navy game formally dedicated Chicago's Soldier Field.*

OPPOSITE BOTTOM: *Army-Navy tradition, circa 1942.*

BELOW: *Mascots meet, 1942.*

TOP: *Michigan coach Bo Schembechler prowling the sideline, no doubt urging his players to beat hated Ohio State.*

ABOVE: *Minnesota vs. Michigan, 1968. Virtually every Big Ten school nurses a rivalry with every other.*

RIGHT: *Michigan's alumni and boosters are the loudest and the proudest in the Big Ten – and the most hated by other Big Ten alums.*

OPPOSITE: *Jubilant and reckless Gator fans tear down the goal post at Florida State's Campbell Stadium after Florida beat State, 13-10, in the annual game for state bragging rights.*

ABOVE: *Alabama's Tyrone King makes an airborne interception of a Georgia pass in 1972.*

LEFT: *Frank Sinkwich, Georgia star, 1941: "Fireball Frankie."*

and the Buckeyes were undefeated going into the game. On the other side of the field, Schembechler was starting freshman quarterback Rick Hewlett, who had virtually no college experience.

A Buckeye field goal was the lone score in the first quarter. John Wangler came off the bench to replace Hewlett as Wolverine signal-caller, and promptly threw a 59-yard touchdown pass to All-American Anthony Carter, Michigan's crack wide receiver.

Schlichter retaliated with a 72-yard drive in eight plays, but had to settle for a field goal. The third period saw another Buckeye drive, and another touchdown. The two-point conversion attempt failed, but Ohio State owned a 12-7 lead.

Now it was Michigan's turn again, with Wangler dropping back to look Anthony Carter's way again, for a 66-yard gain. Moments later, the Wolverines scored and achieved a two-point conversion to surge ahead 15-12.

With only 11 minutes to play in the game, disaster struck Michigan. Set to punt from their own 38-yard line, Michigan's effort was blocked by ten men of Ohio State in a desperate line-of-scrimmage stand. As fans watched in horror, the ball bounced around deep in Michigan's territory until OSU's Todd Bell played Johnny-on-the-spot, picking it up and scooting in to score.

OSU played classic ball-control for the remaining minutes of the game, and left Ann Arbor with their first win in four years – and smelling Roses.

Neighbors feud. Perhaps that's the basis for the rivalry between Alabama (where they invented head-painting, it is rumored) and Geor-

145

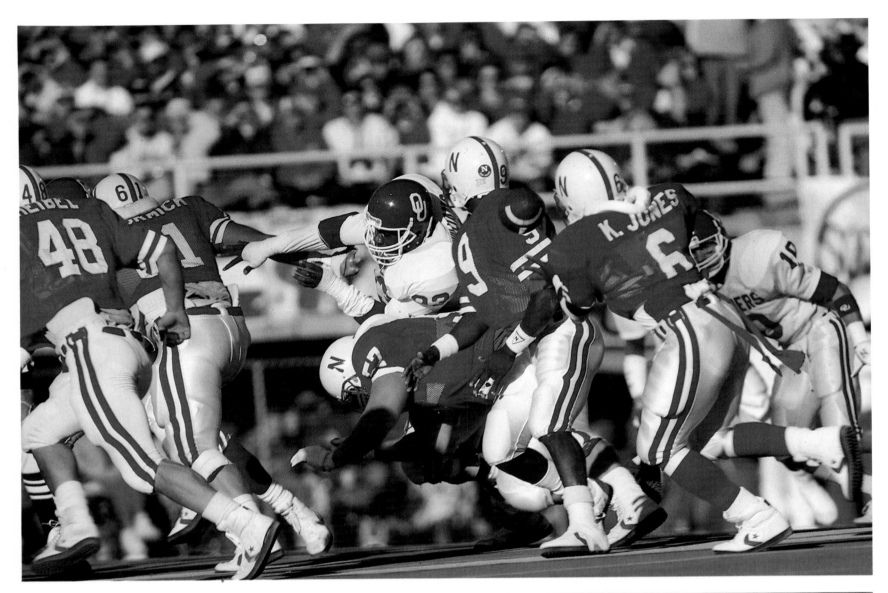

ABOVE: *Color it red: Nebraska and Oklahoma in their annual Big Eight blood feud.*

RIGHT: *Georgia's secret weapon: Herschel Walker steams for the goal line. Walker garnered the 1982 Heisman Trophy for runs like this one.*

OPPOSITE TOP: *"A prison riot with coeds" – the Texas-Oklahoma game.*

OPPOSITE BOTTOM: *The annual contest between Alabama and Auburn is a classic Southern rivalry.*

gia (those Dawgs of war). College football Southern-style is played fiercely. Alabama and Georgia are particularly proud of their status as charter members of the Southern Intercollegiate Athletic Association back in 1894, and of their status among the top 15 winningest college football teams of all time.

In the early decades of the twentieth century, neither Georgia nor Alabama succeeded in rising to the level of football being played in the Midwest or East, but by 1925 the Crimson Tide of Alabama was on the map. That was the year that coach Wallace Wade and backs Pooley Hubert and Johnny Mack Brown went undefeated and untied in 10 games. The Crimson Tide (also called the Red Elephants in those days) was awarded the national championship and the distinction of being the first southern team to travel to Pasadena for the Rose Bowl. They went on to prevail over Washington 20-19.

Georgia had its glory years as well – especially in the early 1940s when Frank Sinkwich, or "Fireball Frankie," as he was known, led the nation in rushing and garnered national attention for the Bulldogs and coach Wally Butts. However, even Sinkwich could not move his favored Georgia team past Alabama that year – but the next season, Sinkwich's Georgia, bolstered by All-American Charley Trippi, did beat Alabama to ruin the Tide's bid for a national championship.

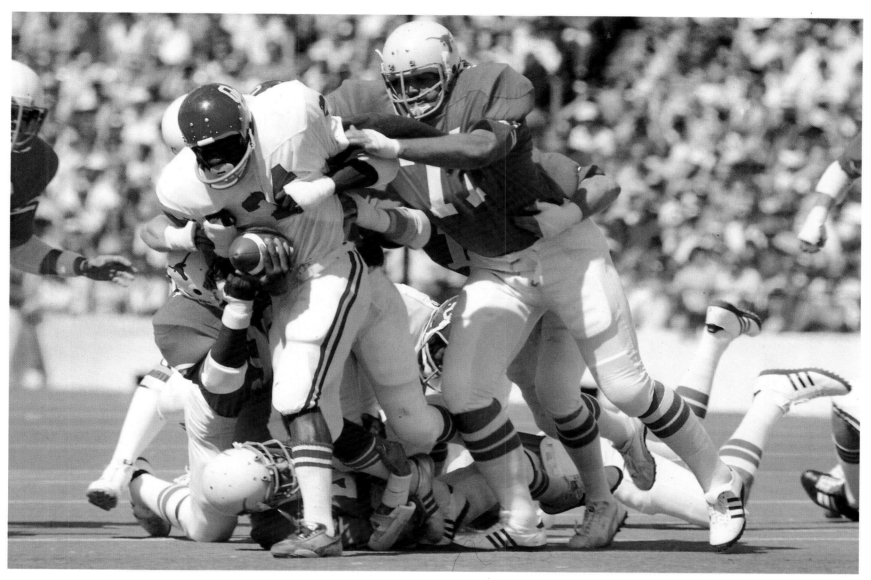

RIGHT: *Treasured Floyd of Rosedale, the travelling trophy which goes to the winner of the annual Iowa-Minnesota game, was modelled after a real pig.*

In the Bear Bryant years at Alabama, perhaps the most sensational contest between the two rivals occurred in 1962. The game marked young Joe Willie Namath's first appearance at Alabama, and the passing wizard with the fragile knees led the Crimson Tide to a stunning 35-0 win over Georgia. But it was off-the-field events which made it so memorable.

An article in the *Saturday Evening Post* sent shock waves through college football by alleging that the game had been fixed – that a telephone conversation between Wally Butts, then Georgia's athletic director, and Bear Bryant had included details of Georgia plays, and other pertinent information. This conversation had allegedly been overheard by an insurance salesman named George Burnett, who gave the story to the *Post*.

The charges were met with lawsuits and decided in court. The case was eventually settled to the overwhelming satisfaction of Butts and Bryant, who had vehemently denied all charges from the beginning. Both coaches were awarded hundreds of thousands of dollars in damages. The two teams did not play each other again until 1972.

Another hiatus in this rivalry occurred from 1978 to 1983, during which, ironically, Alabama captured the national crown in 1978 and 1979, and Georgia was Number 1 the following year with running back extraordinaire, Herschel Walker.

There are certainly other great rivalries in college football: Pittsburgh and Penn State, Tennessee and Vanderbilt, Iowa and Iowa State, Texas and Texas A & M, Alabama and Auburn, Minnesota and Michigan, Minnesota and Iowa, Cornell and Colgate, Missouri and Kansas, and Oklahoma and Nebraska are among the contests which bring fans to their feet each year.

Trophies Are What You Make Them

Sometimes the two teams involved in a classic rivalry are playing for more than just glory and revenge. Sometimes they're playing for a bronze pig. Or an old wooden bucket. Or a special beer keg, or a brass spittoon, or a Little Brown Jug.

Trophies are more than just old antique things that got picked up somewhere along the way and made into treasured items passing between the two schools. They are symbols of the rivalry itself, and an acknowledgment that the rivalry will go on and on, something that can be counted on each year. They also give fraternity pranksters something to steal, hide, ransom or otherwise abuse.

Some particularly old and treasured trophies get passed around in the Big Ten. The Little Brown Jug belongs, each year, to the winner of the Michigan-Minnesota game. Here's how it got started: In the days of Fielding Yost's "Point-A-Minute" Wolverines, the team's water jug,

a rather humble-looking brown piece of earthenware, sat on the sideline for the team's use. After a startling tie in 1903 by an underdog Minnesota team, Yost hustled his dejected players off the field and out of town, leaving the jug behind by mistake. A triumphant Gopher trainer sent a note to his Michigan counterpart, telling him, "If you want the jug back – come and get it!" The old jug has passed to the winner of the game ever since.

The Old Oaken Bucket is a weird-looking item, festooned with bronze letters "I" and "P", denoting the winner each year of the Indiana-Purdue game. This ancient, immense oak keg, goes the story, was used by Morgan's Raiders during the Civil War, as they invaded Indiana's Yankee territory. Hoosier alumni made it into a true war trophy, adding a commemorative plaque.

The bucket has had a colorful history. Once it disappeared for months and was feared lost – until an anonymous tipster contacted Indiana officials and a search party dug the bucket up from the dirt in the basement of the library. Another time, after Indiana had upset Purdue, the bucket disappeared shortly after arrival in Indianapolis. A duped railroad station agent had handed over the souvenir to an "honor guard" of students dressed in Indiana sweaters – who were Purdue partisans in disguise. Of course, the bucket never made it to Indiana's campus, and did not resurface for a long time.

During the 1935 season, Governor Floyd B Olson of Minnesota and Governor Clyde Herring of Iowa made a friendly wager, as politicians often will, on the outcome of that year's Iowa-Minnesota football game – in an effort to ease the tension of what had already become an intense rivalry. After Iowa lost the game 13-6, Herring presented Olson with "Floyd of Rosedale" – a full-blooded champion pig. Floyd was a handsome devil, a brother to "Blue Boy," the prize pig who appeared in the movie *State Fair* (1933).

The real Floyd later settled down to a pig's life in Minnesota, but a bronze replica created by St Paul sculptor Charles Brioscho travels back and forth between the two schools as the treasured prize for the

ABOVE: The Ivy Championship Trophy: a treasured symbol.

BELOW: The modest earthenware jug which goes to the winner of the Minnesota-Michigan game.

LEFT: *The Old Oaken Bucket: a storied history of theft and intrigue between Purdue and Indiana fans.*

ABOVE: *The Indian Princess belonged to the winner of the Dartmouth-Cornell match.*

BELOW: *To the winner of the Wisconsin-Minnesota game, Paul Bunyan's Axe: a fitting symbol of the Northwoods.*

winner. Floyd measures 21 inches long and 15 inches high, and holds a special place in the hearts of Hawkeye and Gopher fans. Cries of "Bring Floyd Home!" often ring out at Iowa-Minnesota games as an inspiration for last year's loser to avenge the loss.

Victory bells of one kind or another pass between several schools. UCLA and USC, Duke and North Carolina, Pacific and San Jose, and Cincinnati and Miami of Ohio, all play for a bell. The Japanese Bell (also called the Enterprise Bell) goes to the Army-Navy winner.

Throughout the years, schools have fought for a variety of in-teresting, idiosyncratic trophies. Illibuck, a wooden turtle of indeterminate origin, goes to the victor of the Ohio State-Illinois game. Minnesota and Wisconsin play for Paul Bunyan's Axe, Florida and Miami of Florida play for the Seminole War Canoe, and Mississippi and Mississippi State vie for the Golden Egg. A Buffalo Head goes to either Colorado or Nebraska each year – and Oklahoma gets a Cowboy Hat if the team beats Texas. Princeton and Rutgers still play for the same rusty old cannon that was in dispute in 1869. Southern Methodist and Texas Christian go after the Old Frying Pan, and on and on.

Robinson's Grambling

There's a small college in northern Louisiana called Grambling, where a coach named Eddie Robinson just keeps on winning football games. Already having won the most games in the history of college football, Robinson is nearing 70, the mandatory retirement age set by Grambling – but he's got a way to go yet.

Robinson began coaching at Grambling at the almost unheard-of age of 22 – when the total enrollment was 320 and the school had just been renamed from the Louisiana Negro Normal and Industrial Institute. Since the early 1950s, Grambling has won an incredible 75 percent of its games.

Although some may contend that Grambling's high degree of success is due largely to its level of opposition and classification as a smaller college (they're currently Division II, in the Southwestern Athletic Conference), they might consider this fact: Eddie Robinson of Grambling has sent as many players to the ranks of professional football as any other college coach. Frank Lewis, Sammy White, Charlie Joiner and Doug Williams have played for the quiet man with the raspy voice and the old-fashioned views.

Each morning, Robinson walks up and down the corridors of the Grambling dorm, ringing his old school bell to make sure all his students make it to their first class. He warns his players to stay away from drugs and loose women, and to get their education. Coaching has been his life, and scores of young men, black and white, are grateful.

RIGHT: *Coach Eddie Robinson counsels a Grambling player during the Oregon State game, 1985.*

BELOW RIGHT: *Quarterback Doug Williams in his Grambling days.*

BELOW: *Robinson with some of his Grambling alums at a 1981 banquet: from left to right, Frank Lewis, Sammy White, Robinson, Charlie Joiner.*

OPPOSITE: *Coach Robinson reacts to a fumble.*

The Big Split: The NCAA Divides

The late 1970s and early 1980s featured the NCAA move to split its Division I teams into two groups: I-A and I-AA. The I-AA Division was comprised of teams that wished to continue playing major college football but did not feel they had the resources, in terms of facilities, recruiting or crowd sizes, to remain with the largest football powers.

Forty schools chose to move to the I-AA Division, including Northeastern, Texas Southern, Idaho, Boston University, Nevada-Reno, Portland State and Northern Iowa. Ninety-seven schools remained in the newly created Division I-A – college football's elite.

As the 1980s dawned, football looked like it was in for another boom decade. More colleges were fielding football teams than ever before. Total crowd sizes, according to NCAA figures, were growing every year. Each year saw more television money, more bowl games, and more revenues for more teams from postseason play. America, with an ever-increasing choice of network and cable TV channels at its disposal, could not get enough of college football.

Yet true fans of the college game were starting to point out some flies in the ointment. News of recruiting violations, under-the-table payments to players, and secret slush funds maintained by booster clubs to influence the most promising high school recruits was hitting the newspapers with increasing regularity.

Injuries were mounting too, as more college stadiums installed artificial turf, and as the players steadily grew larger, stronger and faster in order to compete.

This was not the same game that Pudge Heffelfinger had played, nor was it being played for the same reasons. Answering the challenge of modern times will be the biggest game yet for college football.

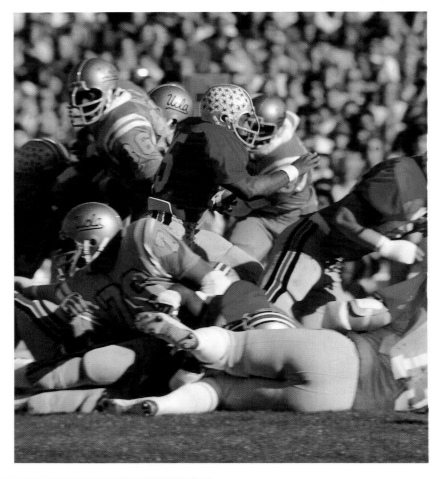

ABOVE: *Archie Griffin made history at OSU by winning two Heismans. Here he is at the 1976 Rose Bowl with UCLA. College football was already becoming big business.*

LEFT: *The PAC-8 became the PAC-10 with the addition of Arizona and Arizona State is 1978. Here, Sun Devils Stadium in Scottsdale.*

OPPOSITE: *Washington's Huskies played in eight consecutive bowl games from 1979 to 1986, including the 1981 Rose Bowl. The NCAA split evened things out between the football haves and have-nots.*

Rebirth of eastern rivalries:

ABOVE: *Princeton and Rutgers celebrate the 1969 100th Anniversary of that first college football game.*

RIGHT: *Cornell's 1986 contest with Brown. The Ivy League is now in Division I-AA.*

OPPOSITE: *Players with futures in the pros, such as Yale's halfback Calvin Hill of the late 1960s, still emerge from I-AA play.*

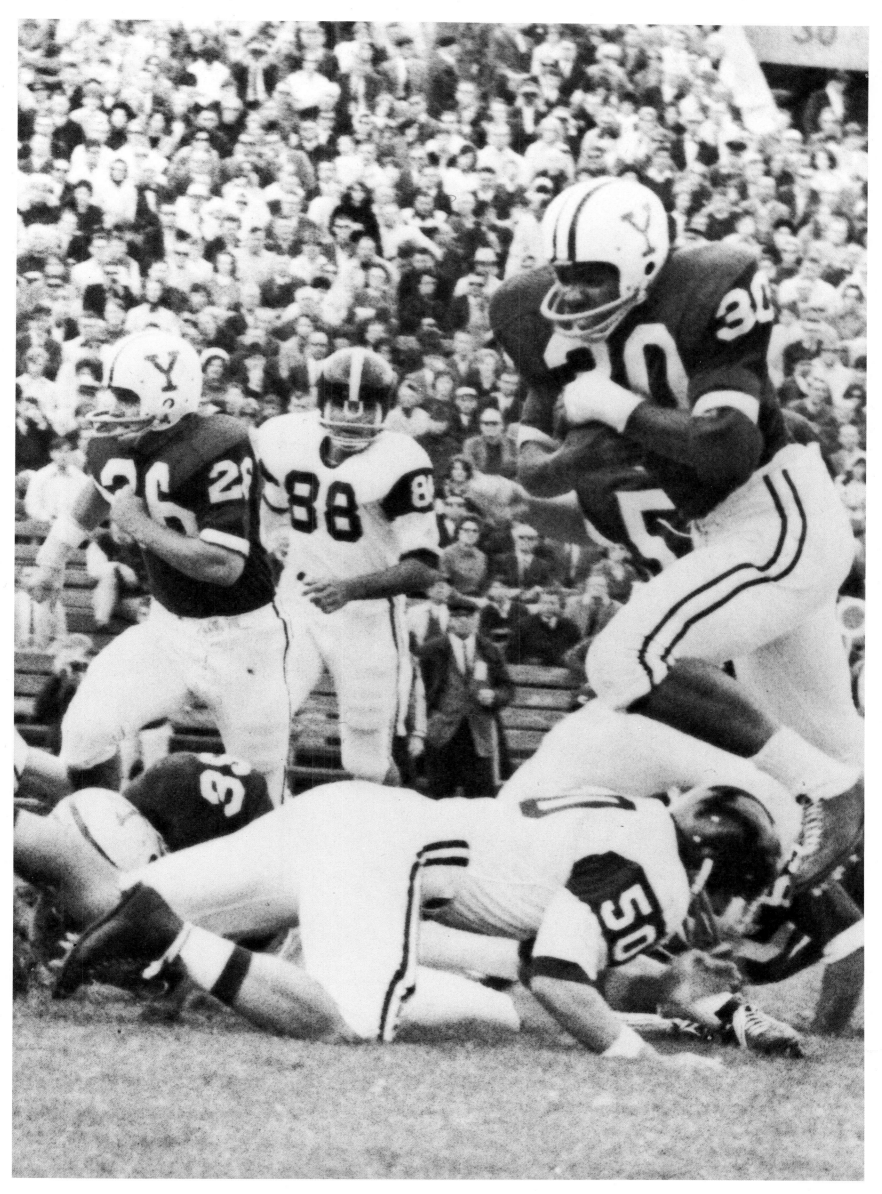

PART IV

The Challenge of Modern Times

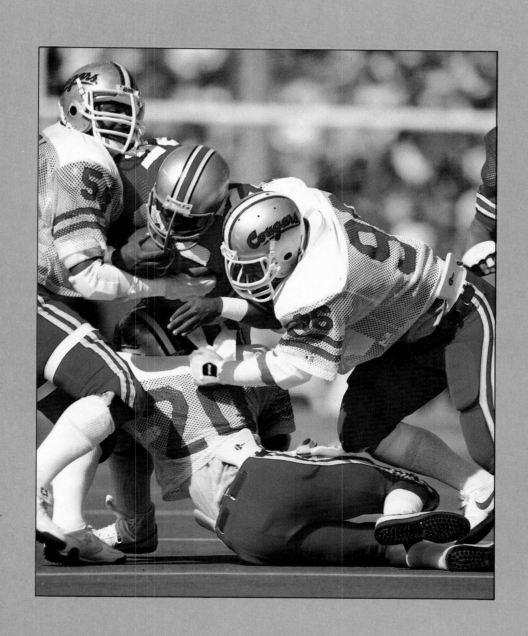

Are They Amateurs?

"Ask the average man on the street what he thinks of college athletics, and he will tell you that schools are making millions of dollars off their athletes, all schools cheat, athletes don't graduate and they are all on drugs," stated the executive director of the NCAA, Richard D Schultz, in a recent interview in the *Sporting News*.

Schultz, who took over the job of top man at the NCAA in 1987 from 36-year director Walter Byers, has a tough job ahead of him. College athletics, and college football most of all, has received more than its share of bad publicity in the 1980s.

The stadiums are still full, the action on the field is thrilling to watch, and American college football is still Number 1. But the influence of professional football, and the unrelenting pressure to rank among the Top 20 in the national polls, has cast a shadow over the efforts of college coaches and athletes.

Is a player strong as a bull naturally, or has he been taking anabolic steroids? Did a team lose a heartbreaker to an underdog conference rival, or did they throw the game for money? Is a young high school star bound for State because of personal loyalty, or thousands in illicit cash and a promise of a new Corvette?

These, and other issues, will have to be addressed by the NCAA and by coaches, players and fans in the years to come. Many feel the root of the problem lies in the very glory of winning football, which has made the game the nation's favorite. So many colleges want a slice of that glory that some school administrations, boosters, coaches and players will do anything to win.

To win, of course, a school must get the best high school players. And that's where the recruiting game comes in. In his book *The Death Of An American Game*, John Underwood talks about college recruiting:

The colleges do not hold player drafts. Instead, they recruit. They allow their coaches to roam the countryside like snake-oil salesmen, trying (sometimes desperately) to win within (and sometimes without) the rules the best players for their schools. . . .

Recruiting in its present form suckles the caste system, helps keep the downtrodden down. The operational word is 'expensive.' Every coach wants the best material, so he can win and go to bowls and get a five-year extension on his contract. It would be un-American to want otherwise. But it is absolute lunacy for 40 or 50 coaches to spend thousands of dollars on phone calls and jetting back and forth across the country to recruit one solitary athlete.

PREVIOUS PAGE: *Washington State vs. Ohio State. As the players have gotten bigger, so have the stakes.*

RIGHT: *The NCAA's new Executive Director, Dick Schultz. He'll be faced with many challenges.*

TOP RIGHT: *Walter Byers, who was Executive Director of the NCAA for 36 years.*

OPPOSITE: *Notre Dame's Father Theodore Hesburgh, who for many years was the living conscience of Fighting Irish athletics.*

TOP: *Northwestern's coach Francis Peay: Can football success coexist with scholarship?*

RIGHT: *Eric Dickerson of SMU on the move. SMU has dropped college football after repeated violations.*

ABOVE: *The price of victory.*

Schultz, who is a former Iowa basketball coach and athletic director himself, has travelled around the country early in his NCAA tenure talking about the problems of using money or other inducements to procure top athletes:

I was in this business for 25 years, and maybe if I had cheated as a coach I would have been a little more successful. But I think as a coach, you've got to live with yourself first. And the first time you offer an athlete something you shouldn't, you are no longer recruiting an athlete. You are buying a witness.

Indeed, former college football players from some of the nation's top programs have written "kiss-and-tell" books or otherwise gone public about recruitment violations they witnessed, or were a party to,

during their college careers.

Some observers even suggest that the whole question of money to college football players be recognized and legalized – why not make college athletes employees of their schools, and pay them as such?

As it stands now, the recognized "payment" made to the athlete at any major school is a full-ride scholarship – in effect, the school pays for the young man's education, and in return he theoretically plays his heart out on the gridiron.

Of course, there are countless examples of individual institutions which still place academics above athletics – and still remain in the top ranks of the college football hierarchy. Notre Dame, Northwestern (returning to competitiveness under coach Francis Peay) and Stanford are among them. Michael Oriard wrote in his 1982 book *The End of Autumn*:

Notre Dame's academic record has been impressive. All of the seniors in my class graduated in four years – as remarkable an accomplishment then as it would be now. When I took over as center during my junior year (1968), our offensive line from tackle to tackle had a 3.4 grade point average. In 1981 it was revealed that over 97 percent of all Notre Dame athletes graduate – as opposed to figures usually half that or much less among major athletic powers . . . .

The emphasis on academics at Notre Dame begins with the president, Father Hesburgh [recently retired], who tells his coaches that losing is permissible but cheating is not. Athletes who are unlikely to survive academically are just not recruited. When Ara Parseghian left as coach in 1975, his proudest boast to Father Hesburgh was not that he had won two national championships but that he could say, 'I'm not leaving any dirt under the carpet.'

Indeed, it may be that strong university administrators and athletic directors, rather than the NCAA, will ultimately be responsible for seeing to it that college football recovers its reputation.

"Maybe we need to develop some type of unilateral agreement on the types of facilities we have and the types of programs we have so we stop trying to keep up with each other," Schultz concludes. "There will be far more schools that operate in the red this year than the black. That tells us if we don't step in and start controlling our own affairs, somebody is going to step in and control them for us."

But change comes slowly to an intensely competitive sport where so much, seemingly, is at stake. When Southern Methodist University recently discontinued college football after repeated NCAA violations had surfaced, the press as well as college football fans across the country termed it "the death penalty."

163

The Elusive National Champ

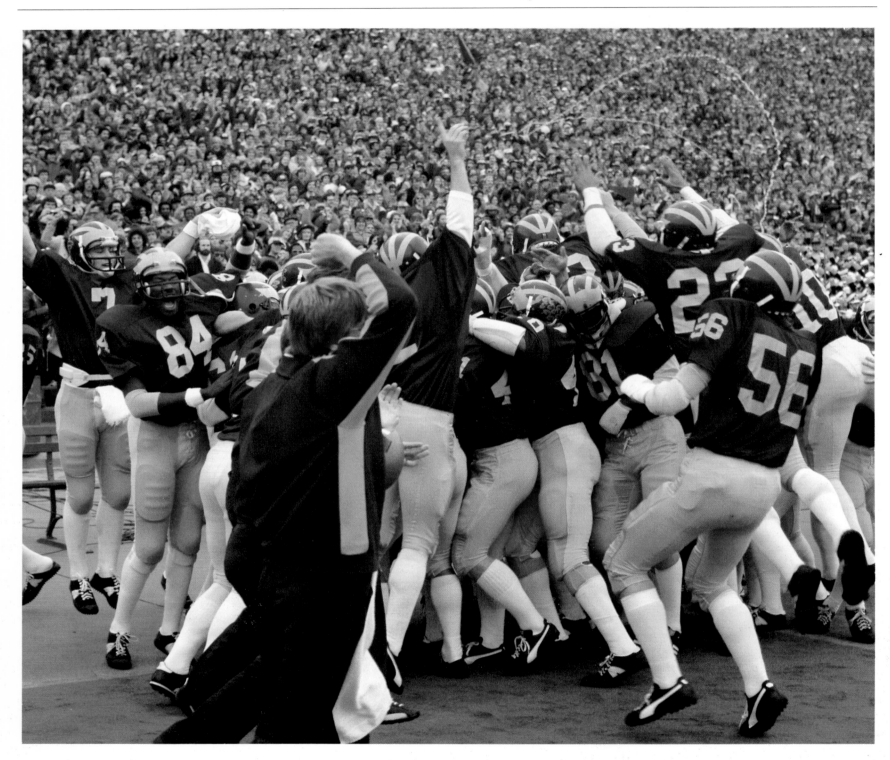

Which is the nation's best football team? That's a question which seems to come up every season, as there has never been a "playoff" system to narrow down to a single game for the national college football championship.

Of course, postseason bowl games provide a measure of championship feel, and certainly the committees which administer each of these postseason games make sure the matchups feature top teams. Usually, at least one bowl game will feature the Number 1-ranked team against the team which is rated Number 2 or Number 3, and the game will be said to be "for the championship." But at the end of the season, the various national polls of sportswriters and coaches must agree who is Number 1 for there to be an undisputed national champion.

Every few years, someone will come up with yet another idea for a postseason tournament to determine a national champion in college football. But although the extra revenue generated would be attractive, and many fans would like to see such a system, the prevailing sen-

ABOVE: *Michigan celebrates a big victory. Are Bowl games enough to settle the question of which team is Number 1?*

OPPOSITE: *Georgia Tech battles USC. Grades take a back seat when you're battling for a Bowl victory in January.*

timent seems to be that the college football season already lasts too long. Some minor bowl games, and the College All-Star game, extend well into January, and the athletes are already behind in their school work, they say.

Also, the logistics of establishing the field, choosing warm-weather sites which still provide neutrality, and dealing with the television networks have ensured that the postseason tournament idea remains just an idea – for now.

Meanwhile, fans of the nation's top teams continue to shout "We're Number 1!" whether it's true or not. Rankings are just rankings – fan spirit confers the championship on many teams.

LEFT: *A Texas Longhorn player rejoices after beating Oklahoma. Each major poll must agree in order to have a national champ at the end of the season.*

OPPOSITE TOP: *The Georgia Bulldogs come ravening out of the locker room to face Penn State in the Sugar Bowl, 1983. Bowl bids mean big bucks for the program.*

OPPOSITE BOTTOM: *Fans bundled against the cold at the Nebraska-Oklahoma game, 1971. Fans and boosters put pressure on teams to win – at all costs.*

Pro Football Beckons

The influence of professional football on the college game, and vice versa, is subtle but profound.

As styles of play change and evolve at the professional level, the trickle-down effect changes the college game too – after all, most college players dream of breaking into the NFL, and the more familiar they are with the current fashion in running versus passing, for instance, the more marketable they will be at draft time.

On the other hand, pro teams have to work with the available college talent – and thus a team in transition may draft a top player with a particular style and build the new strategy around him.

For example, for years it was said that Big Ten quarterbacks, even those drafted in the first round, had a difficult time adjusting to the NFL because they had been schooled in the ground game. They were just handoff artists, said the critics, who couldn't break a game open with flashy passes. The NFL was more likely to draft its quarterbacks from the Big Eight or Southeast country, where the signal-callers knew what throwing the ball was all about.

So pro scouts looked elsewhere for quarterbacks: John Elway was a Stanford standout and now runs the Denver Bronco offense; and Dan Marino of the Miami Dolphins, who went to Pitt of all places, has been hailed as one of the best passers in the NFL. Fighting Irishman Joe Montana fit right in on the San Francisco 49ers. Bernie Kosar of the Cleveland Browns was a University of Miami star. Brigham Young has been known as a good place to grow NFL quarterbacks: From Jim McMahon in the late 1970s to Steve Young in the early 1980s, Brigham Young QBs have gone on to success in the NFL.

However, the past few drafts have seen Big Ten quarterbacks again ascending the NFL lists, as the Grand Old Conference picks up its passing game. Chuck Long of Iowa has found a home with the Detroit Lions, Mike Tomczak of Ohio State backs up McMahon on the Chicago Bears, and it looks like having been a Big Ten quarterback is no longer the stigma it once was.

Southern conferences produce the runners, it seems. Herschel Walker of Georgia and Bo Jackson at Auburn have decimated NFL defenders in pretty much the same way they did in college, and now the South rules the backfield.

A recent article in *Sports Illustrated* commented on the modern trend toward handing off and pitching the ball to running backs in the college game. Whether this started in the pros (because of the lack of passing quarterbacks) or is just a college trend dating back to Walker

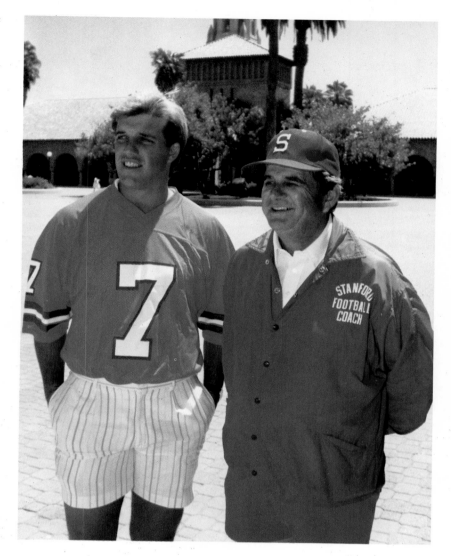

and Jackson is debatable, but the late 1980s finds the running game gaining status.

Sportswriters say it's liberalized blocking rules. It could just be the great running backs have sparked the offenses to be built around the run. Whatever the current trend, the NFL will continue to influence the college ranks, and in turn evolve according to the dictates of this year's draft.

OPPOSITE: *Pitt Panther Dan Marino went on to stand the NFL on its ear with his exceptional passing.*

TOP: *Elway and son: John Elway played for his father Jack at Stanford, and then went on to star as quarterback in Denver Bronco orange.*

LEFT: *Joe Montana. The Fighting Irishman became perhaps the dominant pro quarterback of the 1980s with the San Francisco 49ers.*

169

OPPOSITE: *Rangy blond Chuck Long demolished records at Iowa and now hopes to do the same for the Detroit Lions.*

ABOVE: *Steve Young crashed the NFL after a successful career at Brigham Young.*

LEFT: *Jim McMahon, who directs the Chicago Bears after his own days at BYU, the "Cradle of QBs."*

171

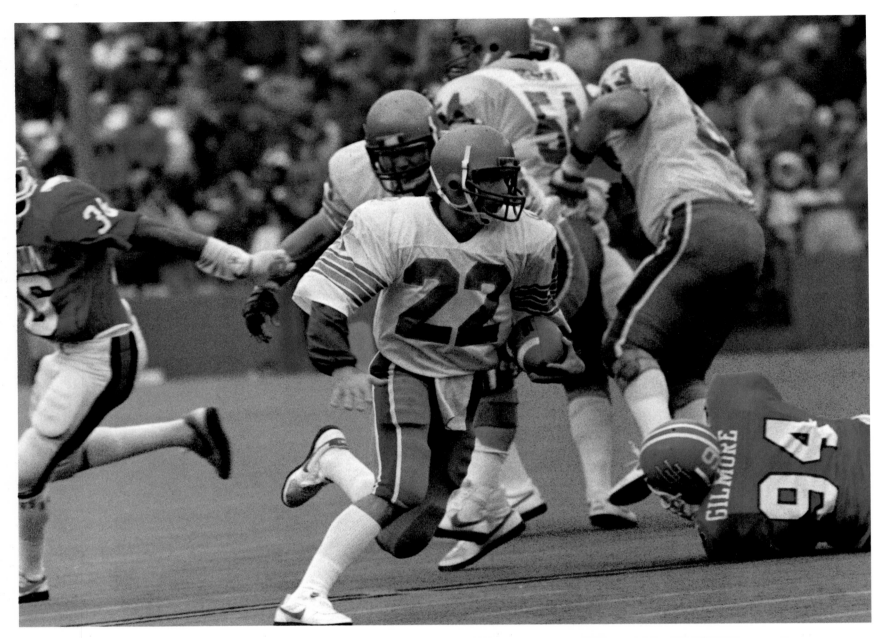

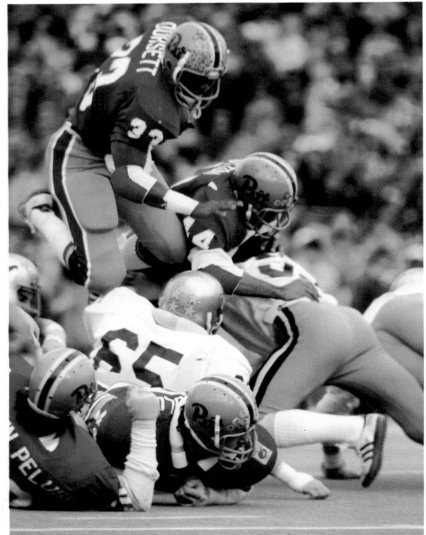

OPPOSITE TOP: *Doug Flutie, the diminutive former signal-caller at Boston College and 1984 Heisman Trophy winner, has proven that the NFL isn't necessarily a big man's domain.*

OPPOSITE BOTTOM LEFT: *Bo Jackson has taken the NFL in stride after his Heisman days at Auburn.*

OPPOSITE BOTTOM RIGHT: *Tony Dorsett, 1976 Heisman winner – another Pitt Panther who made good in the NFL.*

ABOVE: *Marcus Allen played his heart out at USC and won the 1981 Heisman Trophy. Shown here in a 1979 game against Notre Dame, he found success in the pros as well.*

TOP: *Brian Bosworth has brought his hair, mouth, and playing style to the NFL with him from Oklahoma.*

ABOVE: *Mark Harmon at UCLA. The son of Michigan great Tom Harmon, he is now a well-known actor in films and TV.*

RIGHT: *Earl Campbell at Texas, in the 1978 Cotton Bowl. The 1977 Heisman Trophy winner earned fame in the NFL, which another generation of college players would like to emulate.*

ABOVE: *Football runs in the family. Son of legendary Miami Dolphin coach Don Shula, Mike Shula blazed his own trail at Alabama.*

RIGHT: *Navy standout Roger Staubach won the 1963 Heisman, then went on to even greater stardom as quarterback of the Dallas Cowboys.*

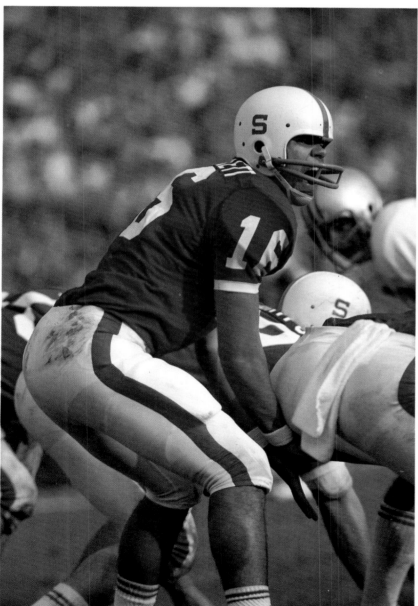

OPPOSITE: *The bruising Dick Butkus at Illinois. The 1964 Heisman runner-up left some big footprints on the Chicago Bears as well.*

TOP LEFT: *Bernie Kosar at Miami in 1984. He took his passing touch into the NFL with him.*

LEFT: *Jim Plunkett at Stanford. He grabbed the 1970 Heisman Trophy away from runner-up Joe Theismann, then stormed the NFL.*

ABOVE: *The Heisman winner for 1983 was Nebraska's Mike Rozier, who ran all the way into the pro ranks.*

179

Independent and Proud Of It

The 1980s have witnessed continuing shifts in the organization of college football at all levels. Besides the six major conferences, consisting of the Atlantic Coast Conference, Big Ten, Big Eight, Pac-10, Southeastern Conference and Southwest Conference, there are other groups for college football fans to watch: the Ivy League; the Mid-American Conference featuring such teams as Miami of Ohio, Ball State, Kent State and Bowling Green; the Western Athletic Conference, with Air Force, Brigham Young, Texas-El Paso and Wyoming, to name a few; the Pacific Coast Athletic Association with Cal State Long Beach, Nevada-Las Vegas and other good smaller schools; and, until recently, the Missouri Valley.

The Missouri Valley had been the forerunner of the Big Eight with Kansas, Missouri, Nebraska and some others. Until the mid-1980s the sprawling conference had drawn attention with a high level of play. Members included Bradley, Creighton, Drake, Illinois State, Indiana State, Southern Illinois, Tulsa, West Texas State and Wichita State. However, in 1985 the Missouri Valley Conference was facing an identity crisis.

BELOW: *Back to football dominance under Coach Lew Holtz is independent Notre Dame.*

RIGHT: *Howard Schnellenberger's University of Miami teams have succeeded independently of any conference. Here he is flanked by Anthony Frederick (left) and QB Jim Kelly (right) after winning the 1981 Peach Bowl.*

OPPOSITE: *Syracuse teams are more than just a preseason test for conference teams like OSU.*

Major independent football powers, clockwise from top left: Tulane, Rutgers, Tulsa, and West Virginia (with Major Harris).

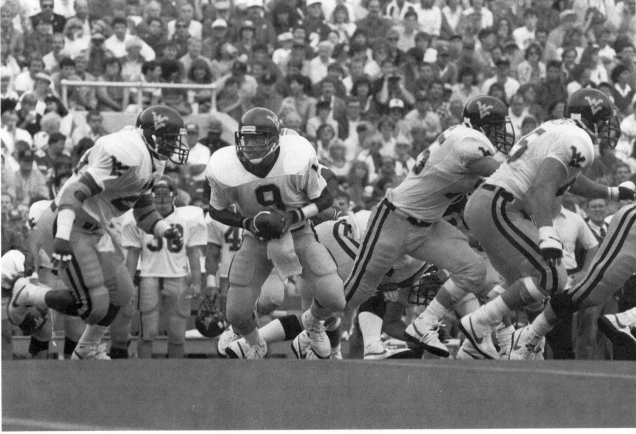

Tulsa and Wichita State wanted to continue competing in Division 1-A and felt they were good enough. But the other teams in the conference were, quite simply, getting killed. And Bradley and Creighton wanted to drop football altogether. So the group broke up on friendly terms after the 1985 season, leaving its former members to compete as independents in either 1-A or 1-AA, as they chose.

Meanwhile, the 1980s may yet be known as the decade of the independents. Penn State under the venerable Joe Paterno, Miami of Florida under Howard Schnellenberger, and Notre Dame returning to its old glory under Lew Holtz, are just a few examples of schools who

are at the very top of college football and yet owe allegiance to no conference. These teams pick their own schedules according to individual rivalries, fan preferences and with an eye toward the national polls. They can play other independents, and are also usually in demand as early-season non-conference "tune-ups" for the Big Ten, Big Eight and other organized conference teams. And they often beat them too!

Other top independents include Tulane, Army, Navy, Colgate, West Virginia, Pitt, Syracuse, Temple and Rutgers. A glance at the Top 20 any Saturday will reveal a few of the mighty independents right in the thick of it.

Football is All-American

LEFT: *Archie Griffin, two-time Heisman winner at Ohio State, waves his diploma over his head in 1976, calling it "the biggest gain of my college career."*

OPPOSITE TOP: *First-round NFL draft choice George Rogers of South Carolina celebrates with New Orleans Saints head coach Bum Phillips.*

OPPOSITE BOTTOM: *Georgia's Herschel Walker signs up with the New Jersey Generals of the USFL.*

An American boy can grow to manhood and on to middle-age and never stop playing football. Autumn will mean football, cheerleaders and glory to him the rest of his life, such a hold can the game have.

Some old players, washed up at 35, can't get used to not hearing the cheering any more. Little kids can get pushed into becoming "killers" in junior high football.

Yet many say the pendulum is starting to swing back. All over the country, youth football leagues are popping up in park districts where all the kids play and no one keeps track of the score. More teams are allowing girls to play touch and flag versions alongside their male schoolmates.

In high school football, equipment is being tested that may bring a new level of safety to the game in the future – helmets, knee braces and, most of all, teaching the kids not to lead with their heads, are all having an effect on reducing injuries.

For those who make it to the college ranks, football is still big business – no doubt about it. But the publicity about recruiting scandals, steroid use and the damage it can do to a young body, and most of all the new importance attached to finishing school, are making college "student-athletes" think twice or three times. An average NFL career, experts say, lasts less than five years. Today's college players know they may just need that college degree – if only to know what to do with the pro contract money.

Academic All-America teams are receiving more recognition, and not just from the NCAA. The student-athlete may once again be a role-model for youngsters.

It remains for college adminstrations, booster clubs, coaches and athletic departments to put college football back into perspective – to view the game as something other than the school's meal ticket, and the athletes as human beings rather than disposable utensils. Winning is not everything.

Americans, with their long history of struggling against adversity and coming out on top, will lust after football glory as long as there are tales left to tell about the Pudge Heffelfingers, the Red Granges and the Jim Thorpes. The game of football has evolved through the decades. But those who love the game must make their voices heard, so that those who run the game will keep some old virtues in mind in the 1990s and beyond.

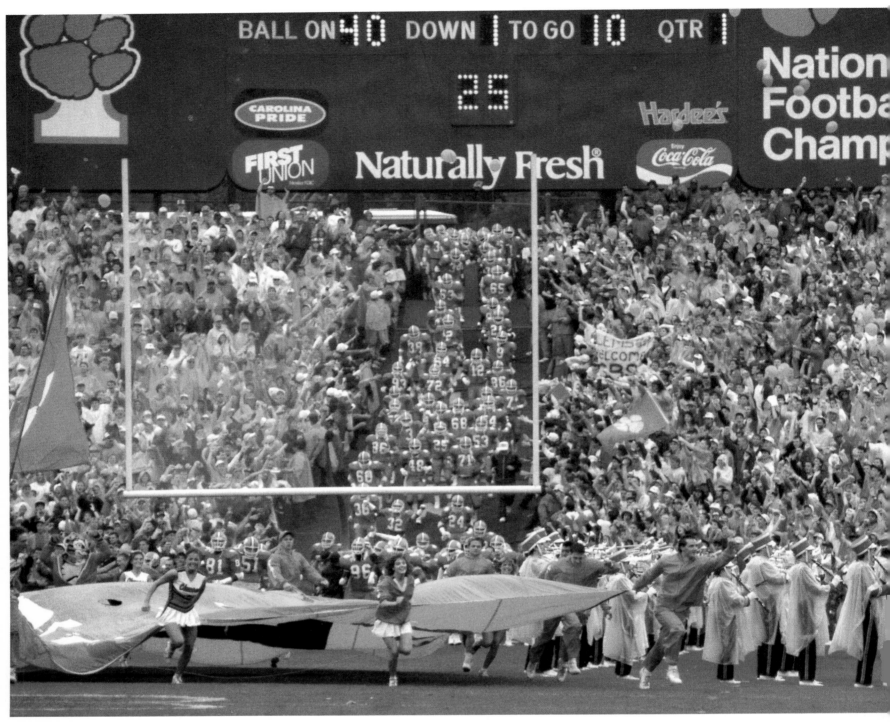

ABOVE: *Clemson pride, 1988-style. Fans are still in love with college football.*

RIGHT: *Texas fans with their infamous Longhorn hand gesture.*

186

RIGHT: *Maryland "Terps" jubilant on the sideline – a sunny day and the whole world is watching.*

ABOVE: *The "Sooner Schooner" – symbol of Oklahoma's pioneer past.*

NEXT PAGE: *A patriotic salute, courtesy of the fan card section at the 1976 Rose Bowl between Ohio State and UCLA. Football is All-American!*

INDEX

Photo Credits

Cover photo: National Football Foundation's College Football Hall of Fame, King's Island, OH 45034/Photo by Richard Norton.

Arizona State University: 154(bottom).
The Bettmann Archive: 10(bottom), 11, 12-13(top), 17(bottom), 18, 20, 22(bottom), 23(bottom), 27(top), 30-31(both), 38-39(both), 46, 48, 50-51(top), 52(top left, bottom), 53(top), 54-55, 59, 66-67, 71(top left, top right), 72, 76(bottom), 77(top), 78-79, 80-81(top), 116(left), 117(top right), 140(bottom), 141(bottom).
Brigham Young University/Mark A. Philbrick: 171(both).
Chance Brockway: 134(bottom left), 181, 182(bottom).
Brompton Picture Library: 9, 10(top), 13(bottom), 23(top), 24, 25, 47(both), 63(bottom), 64(bottom left), 66(left), 80(bottom left), 81(bottom), 116(right), 136(bottom), 140-141(top).
Brown University Archives: 49(top).
Brown University Sports Information Office/Thomas F. Maguire, Jr: 56(bottom left), 129(top).
Cornell University Sports Information Office: 156(bottom).
Dartmouth College Library: 21(bottom), 125(bottom), 151(top right).
O. K. Davis, *Ruston Daily Leader*: 152(bottom left, bottom right).
Malcolm Emmons: 2-3, 6, 76(top), 78(top left), 106(top), 110(top), 113(top, bottom right), 114-115(all three), 118-119(all three), 120, 121(bottom left, bottom right), 122(both), 123(top), 124-125, 125(top), 126-127(both), 128(bottom), 130-131(all four), 133, 134(top right), 135, 138(bottom left, bottom right), 139(both), 142-143(all three), 146-147(all four), 154(top), 159, 162(bottom left), 164-165(both), 166-167(all three), 168, 169(bottom), 170, 172(bottom left, bottom right), 173, 174-175(all three), 176-177(both), 178-179(all four), 180(left), 186(top), 187(both), 188-189, 190.
Georgia Tech Sports Information Department: 101(top).
Harvard Sports News Bureau: 16, 28-29, 106(bottom left).
Harvard University Archives: 117(top left).
Iowa State Historical Society: 90(bottom right).
Kevin Knepp Studio, Inc: 123(bottom), 161.
Library of Congress: 35(top).
NCAA: 160(both).
National Football Foundation & Hall of Fame: 102(top).
Northwestern University: 106(bottom left), 117(bottom), 162(top left).
NYPL Picture Collection: 15, 17(top right), 34(bottom), 35(bottom).
Ohio State University Photo Archives: 74(left), 99(bottom left), 132(bottom).
Princeton University Office of Athletic Communications: 12(bottom), 14-15, 27(bottom), 29(top right), 52(top right), 99(bottom right), 150(top), 156(top).
Purdue University: 108(bottom right), 151(left).
Rutgers University/Jim Turner: 183(top).
SMU Sports Information: 163.
Springer/Bettmann Film Archive: 85(bottom right).

Stanford University Libraries, Department of Special Collections and University Archives: 33(top).
Stanford University Sports Information: 68, 88(bottom), 89(left), 169(top).
Syracuse University: 99(top).
TCU Sports Information: 104(left).
Tulane University Athletic Department: 182(top).
UPI/Bettmann Newsphotos: 32(bottom left), 33(bottom), 36(left), 45, 51(bottom left), 53(bottom), 58(center, bottom left), 60(right), 61(top), 62, 65, 69(both), 70, 71(bottom right), 73(both), 74-75(top), 75(top right), 77(bottom), 81(top right), 83, 84(all three), 85(top, bottom left), 86(top left), 90(bottom left), 91, 92-93(all three), 94-95(all three), 97(both), 102-103, 104-105, 107(top), 112(bottom right), 128(top), 129(bottom), 132(top), 144-145(all three), 152(top), 153, 172(top), 180(right), 184-185(all three).
USF&G Sugar Bowl: 78(bottom left).
University of Alabama: 58(top right), 148.
University of Illinois: 41(both), 61(bottom).
University of Illinois Archives, Record Series: 63(top).
University of Iowa Photo Services: 1, 90(top), 98(left).
University of Kansas: 108(top), 109.
University of Maryland, Department of Intercollegiate Athletics: 100, 101(bottom left, bottom right).
University of Michigan Athletic Department: 36(right), 37(top), 74-75(bottom), 86(bottom), 88(top), 150(bottom).
University of Michigan, University Relations: 102(bottom).
University of Minnesota Archives: 86(top right), 87(both), 149.
University of Minnesota, Department of Men's Athletics: 151(bottom right).
University of Missouri Sports Archives: 89(right), 107(bottom), 108(bottom left).
University of Nebraska: 56(bottom right).
University of Notre Dame Archives: 22(top), 42-43, 49(bottom), 50(bottom), 51(bottom right).
University of Notre Dame Sports Information Office: 64(top right), 96.
University of Oklahoma Sports Information Department: 110-111(bottom), 111(top), 112(top, bottom left), 113(bottom left).
University of Oregon: 56-57(top).
University of Pennsylvania Sports Information: 21(top), 32(top right), 34(top), 40(left).
University of Texas, Austin/Bob Daemmrich: 186(bottom).
University of Tulsa Athletic Department: 183(bottom).
University of Washington: 57(bottom), 155.
University of Wisconsin, Madison Archives: 43(right), 98(right).
Urbana Free Library: 60(left).
Wake Forest Sports Information Department/Bugs Barringer: 58(bottom left).
Yale Sports Publicity: 40(right), 121(top right), 136(top), 137, 157.
Yale University Library: 17(top left), 19, 26, 138(top).

Acknowledgements

The author and publisher would like to thank the following people who helped in the preparation of this book: Mike Rose, designer; Jean Martin, editor; Rita Longabucco, picture editor; and Elizabeth A. McCarthy, indexer.